T0054241

Faithful foot soldiers

The religious right is gaining ground, and free expression cannot survive in its shadow, writes **Jemimah Steinfeld**

YOU'VE READ THE story countless times: the numbers attending a religious institution are diminishing each year. From headlines like "Religion could disappear by 2041" to articles on empty gothic cathedrals and churches turned into nightclubs, the message is clear: the "Nones" – those who have no religious affiliation – are multiplying.

This might be true, but it's happening in tandem with a different trend (and maybe even *because* of the Nones) – the re-emergence of a politically charged, religious right.

Consider just these few examples: a loose coalition of theologically and politically conservative faith groups successfully pushed for the overturning of Roe vs Wade in the USA last year; in January, Pakistan extended its already harsh blasphemy laws; this August, Denmark proposed a law to make improper treatment of the Koran or the Bible a criminal offence punishable by up to two years in jail; a fast-growing group of religious conservatives allied with Israel's Prime Minister Benjamin

Netanyahu is currently trying to neuter the country's Supreme Court.

A binary of "religion bad, no religion good" would be inaccurate – scripture can promote tolerance and injustice happens in the name of atheism, too (just look at North Korea). Still, it is a sad reality of today that there are many who, in the name of faith, are preaching and imposing intolerance, and the direction of travel is not good.

We explore all of this in the Autumn issue. While the religions are different, they all bear a strong family resemblance. Embattlement is at the core, with followers engaged in a conflict with enemies whose values seem inimical to theirs. Identities are built around a reclamation of certain doctrines and practices of the past. These meld with the best tools of modernity and appeal to modern ideals of religious freedom. Here, though, religious freedom is enlisted to support an antidemocratic project. Free expression is lost.

In the special report, Rebecca Root charts the increased imposition of

blasphemy laws around the world, talking to some of the victims, including the wife of a man who is in jail in Nigeria serving a 24-year sentence. From India, Salil Tripathi talks about how even Hollywood film Oppenheimer has caused offence in the increasingly Hindu nation. Kaya Genç writes on the bitter legacy of the Salman Rushdie affair and the secular foundation still feeling the heat in Turkey. Experts on the religious right – author Margaret Atwood and journalist Katherine Stewart – offer their take on what is happening and why.

"The church must be reminded that it is not the master or the servant of the state, but rather the conscience of the state," Martin Luther King Jr. said. Let this report be a reminder.

Outside the special report, we have something else very special – a new story from the esteemed playwright Ariel Dorfman. A tale within a tale, borrowing characters from Dorfman's other work, it's very meta, as the kids would say, and has a murder mystery at the core. Dorfman's story is one of two pieces to mark the 50th anniversary of Augusto Pinochet's coup in Chile and the bloodshed that ensued. The other looks into how the general's popularity remains stubbornly resilient today. ✖

Jemimah Steinfeld, editor-in-chief

52(03):1/1|DOI:10.1177/03064220231201266

Facism's modus operandi

Introducing our cover artist

OUR COVER ARTIST, who is based in South Asia, wishes to go by the name Khan for safety reasons. Khan told Index that censorship is ever-present for them. "Personally it plays into

a paranoia and fear that any action you take could be misconstrued in any number of ways and have dire consequences. It's akin to walking on egg shells while blindfolded," said Khan.

Of the cover image Khan said "the illustration takes a lot of inspiration from political and journalistic cartoons." Khan continued: "There was a strong sense to

depict the destruction that comes from an authoritarian "right" that looks to exert power over minorities and liberties, as has always been the case for a fascist 'modus operandi'".

CONTENTS

Comment

Culture

INDEXONCENSORSHIP.ORG

CHIEF EXECUTIVE
Ruth Anderson

EDITOR-IN-CHIEF
Jemimah Steinfeld

ASSISTANT EDITOR
Katie Dancey-Downs

EDITOR-AT-LARGE
Martin Bright

ASSOCIATE EDITOR
Mark Frary

ART DIRECTOR
Matthew Hasteley

EDITORIAL ASSISTANT
Francis Clarke

SUB EDITORS
Adam Aiken, Tracey Bagshaw, Jan Fox, Sally Gimson

CONTRIBUTING EDITORS
Kaya Genç, Emily Couch, Danson Kahyana, Salil Tripathi

HEAD OF POLICY & CAMPAIGNS
Jessica Ní Mhainín

POLICY & CAMPAIGNS OFFICER
Nik Williams

DEVELOPMENT OFFICER - FUNDRAISING & EVENTS
Ujala Syed

DIRECTORS & TRUSTEES
Trevor Phillips (Chair), Kate Maltby (Vice Chair), Anthony Barling, Andrew Franklin, James Goode, Helen Mountfield, Elaine Potter, Mark Stephens, Nick Timothy

PATRONS
Margaret Atwood, Simon Callow, Steve Coogan, Brian Eno, Christopher Hird, Jude Kelly, Michael Palin, Matthew Parris, Alexandra Pringle, Gabrielle Rifkind, Sir Tom Stoppard, Lady Sue Woodford Hollick

ADVISORY COMMITTEE
Julian Baggini, Jeff Wasserstrom, Emma Briant, Ariel Dorfman, Michael Foley, Conor Gearty, AC Grayling, Lyndsay Griffiths, William Horsley, Anthony Hudson, Natalia Koliada, Jane Kramer, Jean-Paul Marthoz, Robert McCrum, Rebecca MacKinnon, Beatrice Mtetwa, Julian Petley, Michael Scammell, Kamila Shamsie, Michael Smyth, Tess Woodcraft, Christie Watson

The Index

52(03):4/10|DOI:10.1177/03064220231201267

A round-up of events in the world of free expression from Index's unparalleled network of writers and activists

Edited by
MARK FRARY

PICTURED: Ecuador's
Interior Minister Juan
Zapata (hidden) and
police commanders
give a report on
arrests regarding
the assassination
of Ecuadorean
presidential candidate
Fernando Villavicencio
in the capital Quito,
on 10 August 2023

The Index

ELECTION WATCH

FRANCIS CLARKE keeps an eye on the world's poll booths

1. Netherlands

NOVEMBER 2023

General elections in the Netherlands are due to be held a year early in November 2023 after a collapse of the ruling coalition government consisting of the VVD, CDA, D66 and ChristenUnie parties. The collapse was due to ministers disagreeing on measures to reduce the number of close family members able to travel to join those already granted refugee status. The failure to agree comes after a big shock in the country's provisional elections in March, when the Farmer-Citizen Movement, a right-wing populist party that has seen support from Donald Trump and Marine Le Pen, won 20% of the vote. It was initially set up as a movement that disagreed with proposals for tackling nitrogen emissions. The party is now the largest in the

Upper House of Parliament, which has the power to block legislation from the Lower House, to be elected in November.

2. Democratic Republic of Congo

DECEMBER 2023

A group of Congolese Tutsi were guarded by armed police in the eastern town of Nyangezi in April as they registered to vote in the country's upcoming general election on 20 December 2023. They were being attacked by Wazalendo, translated as 'patriots' in Swahili, as part of a campaign of threats and violence aimed at preventing the Tutsi from voting due to ethnic divisions. Martin Fayulu, leader of the opposing Engagement for Citizenship and Development party, believes it's part of a plan by President Felix Tshisekedi to take power away from the Congolese people. This includes unconstitutionally handpicking judges and members of the independent Electoral Commission, and failing to reform unfair electoral laws. Foreign observers and media alleged the result of the previous election in 2019 was rigged in Tshisekedi's favour, and that leaked full voting data showed that Fayulu had won. The African Union, which facilitates pan-African unity across its 55 member countries, went as far as calling for the elections to be suspended.

3. Mali

FEBRUARY 2024

Originally due in February 2022, Mali's general election is now expected to be held in February 2024 following years of political turmoil. After leading the coup that ousted President Ibrahim Boubacar Keïta in February 2020, then vice-president Colonel Assimi Goita led

CLOCKWISE FROM LEFT: Malian interim President Assimi Goita; Congolese President Felix Tshisekedi; Dutch Prime Minster Mark Rutte

Free speech in numbers

6.3 Billions of dollars spent on "sportswashing" by Saudi Arabia since early 2021 according to an analysis by The Guardian newspaper

10 Number of years spent in detention by Egyptian activist Ahmed Douma before he was pardoned by the president Abdel Fattah al-Sisi in August 2023. Douma was a key figure in the 2011 uprising that toppled Hosni Mubarak

19 Number of years of additional sentence handed to Alexey Navalny in August on extremism charges which the leading Putin opponent says is "politically motivated"

3 The number of days it took X (formerly Twitter) to remove a post calling the Holocaust a "fairytale" after initially saying the tweet did not break its safety policies

1,000 Number of days that former Index colleague Andrei Aliaksandrau will have spent in prison in Belarus on 9 October

a second coup in 2021 to take power himself. Despite agreeing to a timetable for fair elections in February 2022, Kéïta has continuously extended his rule. Malians approved changes to the constitution in a referendum this June, which the military rulers said will pave the way to a return to civilian rule. However, opponents say an unelected government has no right to hold such an important referendum. There are also concerns many Malians can't vote in the upcoming election, because northern parts of the country are ruled by armed groups linked to al-Qaeda and ISIL. ✖

PEOPLE WATCH

FRANCIS CLARKE highlights the stories of human rights defenders under attack

Sepideh Gholian

IRAN

On 10 July the Iranian court of appeals upheld a two-year prison sentence issued to Iranian labour rights activist Sepideh Gholian. The sentencing comes three months after she was arrested for treason as a result of video footage on social media showing her protesting the mandatory hijab law by shouting: "Khamenei, the tyrant, we will bury you in the ground". The video was recorded just hours after Gholian was released from four years in prison on similar treason charges.

Siti Zabedah Kasim

MALAYSIA

Human rights lawyer and activist Siti Zabedah Kasim survived an assassination attempt on 21 July after a mechanic discovered an improvised explosive device behind the tyre of her car during a service in Bangsar, Malaysia. Kasim has defended the Orang Asli Indigenous communities fighting for their land rights against mining and logging activities in Peninsular Malaysia. She is also a prominent advocate for the LGBTQI+ community in the country.

Yanina Sokolova

UKRAINE

Ukrainian journalist Yanina Sokolova, an outspoken critic of Russia's ongoing invasion of her country, was added by the Russian Ministry of Internal Affairs to its most wanted list of terrorists and extremists on 7 August. It states Sokolova is sought under a specific (but does not say which) article of the Criminal Code. Sokolova responded by stating: "Well, thank God. I have begun to worry whether my Russophobia was lacking."

Lu Siwei

CHINA

On 28 July, Chinese human rights defender Lu Siwei was detained by Laotian authorities near the Thai border. Due to fly to the USA, his last known sighting was at an immigration centre, where he was told he would be deported to China. Before disbarment, Lu Siwei was a lawyer based in the Sichuan province. He aided victims of human rights violations and focused on issues around free expression, arbitrary detention and enforced disappearances.

Index launches new report on Chinese funding of European universities

Academic freedom in Europe is the latest issue facing a threat from China

Index has published a new report that investigates the extent Chinese money is being used to fund European universities and the extent is it eroding academic freedom in the process.

A survey carried out for the report, At what cost?, found that 52% of academics believed that the Chinese Communist Party posed a threat to academic freedom.

"There is limited direct intervention but there is widespread self-censorship," one survey respondent from the UK explained.

European universities have become increasingly international over the last decade, fostering relationships with researchers, institutions, private companies and students around the world. While academic internationalisation provides many opportunities, it also presents challenges.

"European academia must recognise that vulnerability to authoritarian and illiberal interference is an undeniable reality in the contemporary context of globalised knowledge production," the European Commission said in a working document published last year. "Risks encountered in this context crystallise as threats to the principles of academic freedom and integrity."

The report is the latest chapter in Index's Banned by Beijing campaign, which has also looked

at Confucius Institutes, the targeting by China of the families of exiled activists and efforts to supress artistic freedom beyond the country's borders.

The Index

TECH WATCH

THE RUSSIAN DOING THINGS DIFFERENTLY

Pavel Grata launched a VPN to help fellow Russians access information freely. It is little wonder the authorities have tried to stop him

Visit the vibrant yellow website of the virtual private network provider Deeprism and you are immediately faced with a mission statement. "Respect for rights. Openness. Accessibility."

If this sounds like the musings of a Silicon Valley tech evangelist, you could not be more wrong. Deeprism is the work of former fashion blogger Pavel Grata from Kaliningrad, a Russian exclave between Poland and Lithuania.

Grata, who developed Deeprism working largely alone, told Index: "I am just an ordinary citizen, not an IT company or Superman. I do everything possible so that anyone anywhere in the world can use an anonymiser, proxy and VPN for free and without unnecessary registrations."

Anonymisers and VPNs are some of the most commonly used tools by those trying to share the truth of what is happening in authoritarian regimes. An anonymiser hides your internet address; a VPN goes further and also encrypts the information passing to and from the internet. They are widely used by many as a way to access independent news media and social media platforms. Little wonder then that authoritarian leaders often try to outlaw their use.

Grata, who ran the fashion blog Ikona Russia, launched a free anonymiser called Snowdenway in 2016, followed a year later by the Deeprism VPN. The authorities were quick to notice his work and in various court cases in 2016 and 2017 the authorities

argued that Snowdenway was an extremist organisation.

Grata's sites were attacked with distributed denial of service and vulnerability attacks, which he claims were the work of Russian authorities.

"During this time, I was threatened, physically abused and pressurised over my views," said Grata, who was forced to stop his blog. The threats against Grata took a darker turn that year.

"Free Internet was always a threat to the Kremlin, so I became the object of the [secret service] FSB's close attention, and then their victim. On 27 January 2017, I was admitted to hospital with suspected use of substances against me, the clinical effects of which fit the use of toxic compounds in non-lethal doses."

In 2017, Putin's government passed legislation that criminalised using VPNs to access "unlawful content". It did not mean that using Deeprism and other VPNs was suddenly illegal but meant only VPNs approved by the Russian government – namely those that blocked content that Russia did not want its citizens to see – were allowed.

The VPN providers – many of which are outside Russia – have not always meekly accepted the bans and have made greater efforts to ensure their services remain available to people everywhere, including in Russia.

"Any popular VPN has been blocked at least once in Russia," said Grata. "Today, I don't promise you uninterrupted service but Deeprism is

available on all continents. Considering the ongoing confrontation between NATO and Russia, guaranteeing functionality for Russian users is becoming increasingly challenging."

The launch of Putin's 'special military operation' in Ukraine spurred many Russians to use a VPN for the first time to get access to uncensored news from the frontline. According to the Atlas VPN Adoption Index, VPN downloads in Russia jumped from 12.6 million in 2021 to 33.5 million in 2022.

On 31 July this year, Putin's government signed into law amendments to legislation on information and communication that, while they still have not banned VPNs, have made telling people how to use them a crime. Russian platforms must also record the true identities of users of their services.

"It's evident that the burden will soon fall on the shoulders of Russian internet service providers," said Grata. "They'll have to engage in blocking by IP, port, domain, and traffic signature. It's also evident that the authorities will strengthen control. For now, they've launched advertising warning about the risks of using VPNs. Most users haven't been deterred by these videos."

Given the threats to his life, it's reasonable to ask Grata why he does it.

"I do this because I think it is necessary," he told Index. "Every time I faced pressure, I came up with a new way forward. I did everything almost alone and completely free of charge. Two people who helped and advised me in this area simply turned away from me because they were worried about their lives and are afraid of retribution."

"Now I want only one thing - that the world does not turn away. Yes, I am Russian, but I have never been ashamed of what I do, although at any moment it could cost me my life."

World In Focus: Niger

A military coup shook Niger in July in a part of the world that is already turbulent and unstable. Human rights and free expression are under threat

1. Tamou
In October 2022, the Niger army was accused of unlawfully killing artisanal gold miners using air strikes in the southern village Tamou, which borders Burkina Faso. It followed an attack by an armed group against a police station that killed two police officers and wounded one. The government announced that seven people were killed and 24 people were wounded in a communiqué and denied any unlawful killings had been carried out. In December, after carrying out investigations the National Human Rights Commission announced the airstrike targeted the arms depot of an armed group close to the mining site, which killed 11 individuals, and was followed by a mop-up operation that wounded 25 individuals including civilians.

2. Niamey
In August, Niger's President Mohamed Bazoum was placed under house arrest by the presidential guard and other ministers from his government detained. The guard's commander general Abdourahamane Tchiani appeared afterwards on state-run television and declared himself the head of a transitional government before suspending Niger's constitution. Since then, reports have emerged that Bazoum is living off dry rice and pasta in the presidential palace while neighbouring Nigeria, which supplies much of the electricity to its neighbour, has cut off supplies. Water supplies had also been reported as cut. Bazoum and his ministers have been given no access to legal support or been provided with no reasons for their arrests. Amnesty International said that anyone arrested has the right to know the reasons for their arrest, to have access to a lawyer, to be brought before a judge within a reasonable time and to challenge the legality of their detention.

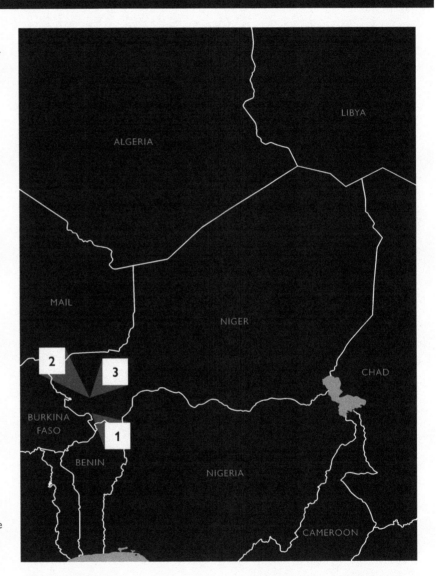

3. Niamey
On 20 August, Niger's military leader Tchiani proposed a three-year transition of power. The announcement was condemned by the Economic Community of West African States, which has been trying to negotiate with the junta. The organisation says it is ready to send troops into Niger to restore constitutional order.

On 22 August, the African Union suspended Niger from its membership and called for the immediate and unconditional release of President Bazoum and other detainees. The Union also said it strongly rejected any external interference by any actor outside the continent in the peace and security affairs in Africa, including engagements by private military companies, a likely reference to Russia's Wagner Group.

The Index

MY INSPIRATION

AN AGONY TRANSFORMED

The persecution of Uyghurs has been too close to home for **RUSHAN ABBAS**, forcing her to fight back harder

ABOVE: Rushan Abbas campaigning for the release of her sister

ERIE SATELLITE IMAGES of a sprawling network of internment camps in Xinjiang gave a new insight into the plight of Uyghurs in 2021. Footage of the gargantuan prisons followed, as did videos of 're-education'. The treatment of Uyghurs in China has been classed as a genocide, and Uyghur activist Rushan Abbas knows about the violations all too well.

From leading student pro-democracy demonstrations in Xinjiang, Abbas took her activism to the USA and created the first Uyghur association in the country.

She's been broadcast across Radio Free Asia, had the ear of Congress and been the voice for Uyghurs in Guantanamo in need of translation. In recent years she has devoted herself completely to activism, founding the Nobel Peace Prize-nominated Campaign

for Uyghurs in 2017, working globally to stop the persecution. Here she writes about her sister, an inspiring figure who is one of the regime's victims.

* * *

When I try to explain my connection with my sister, Gulshan, the verse "For there is no friend like a sister," comes to mind. There are nights when I lie awake, yearning for her presence, wanting to share the intricacies of our transformed lives – the aging, the children growing up, the unravelled plans.

Graduating from Xinjiang Medical University in 1985 marked the beginning of Gulshan's journey as a physician.

Leaving my homeland in 1989 for the USA was my step towards pursuing post-graduate education and change for our people. Knowing Gulshan was there caring for our parents gave me solace.

She has an unwavering dedication to family and her patients. I remember when I welcomed my child into the world and became a mother, she dropped everything to stand by me for months. She made me know that she would always be there for me.

News of worsened conditions in our homeland reached the States. In 2018, after I voiced concerns publicly about my husband's missing family, the CCP (Chinese Communist Party) retaliated by abducting Gulshan. The Beijing regime took her as a hostage for my activism as an American citizen. It's been five years since she was taken.

The agony of not knowing Gulshan's fate has shaped me into a person I never could have imagined. It transformed my life's purpose – from corporate career-driven aspirations to a relentless full-time activist. I doubled-down my efforts to speak out for my people's suffering and expose the CCP's genocidal crimes. I am fuelled everyday by the hope that my actions will someday reunite us. The thought of her in a dim cell, a victim of China's tyranny, shattering me. She taught me empathy and compassion. This guides me through the darkest moments of my journey with resilience. I pray each day that she is staying strong and she is staying alive. ✖

Rushan Abbas is a Uyghur-American activist and founder of Campaign for Uyghurs

FEATURES

"We had the carpet made to remind everyone
that Holy Week was not holy, that it was tainted
by all the blood that had been spilled"

JIMENA LEDGARD | POLICING SYMBOLISM | P.37

Oiling the wheels of injustice

Saudi Arabia splashes oil money to hide its human rights record, which is going from bad to worse. **FRANCIS CLARKE** and **MARK FRARY** investigate

SAUDI ARABIA IS using its vast oil and gas wealth to fund a global charm offensive that the country hopes will help silence critics of its human rights record. The country has been scrambling to rebuild its reputation since the 2018 murder of the journalist Jamal Khashoggi in Turkey, a crime the Director of National Intelligence concluded was ordered by Saudi Crown Prince Mohammed bin Salman, known as MBS (**tinyurl.com/saudiODNI**).

Khashoggi's murder is the most striking demonstration of MBS and his family's attempts to crack down on protest, but Saudi Arabia's disregard for human rights runs far deeper. Research carried out by Index reveals that over

LEFT: Emmanuel Macron receives the Crown Prince of the Kingdom of Saudi Arabia, Mohammed Bin Salman Bin Abdulaziz Al-Saoud, at the Elysee Palace, March 2022

the past few years hundreds of human rights activists and other opponents of the regime have been handed sentences ranging up to 50 years by the country's Specialised Criminal Court (SCC). Some have even been given the death sentence.

Their "crimes" involve peaceful protest against the actions of Saudi's rulers or simply posting messages of support for other human rights defenders on social media. The country's notorious levels of secrecy over its internal workings means it is almost impossible to secure details of court

cases, the trial process and sometimes even the names of those involved. The information that does emerge from the country makes for shocking reading.

The SCC was set up in 2008, with its original function being to handle the trials of people involved in terrorist attacks linked to al Qaeda. Following protests in 2011-12 kindled by the Arab Spring movement, the SCC began handling the cases of peaceful activists whose views differed from those of the country's rulers.

Since then, the actions of the SCC have drawn widespread criticism from around the world. Human Rights Watch called for its abolition in 2012, saying, "Trying Saudi political activists as terrorists merely because they question abuses of government power demonstrates the lengths the Saudi government will go to suppress dissent."

MBS has also consolidated his control of the SCC. According to an Amnesty International report in 2017 several SCC judges were arbitrarily arrested as part of a broader crackdown on civil society. This led to the consolidation of prosecutorial powers and intelligence agencies in the hands of King Salman bin Abdulaziz al Saud and MBS. Some 110 judges of various ranks were promoted and brought in by the King.

Most of the trials that take place in the SCC are for charges relating to Saudi Arabia's terrorism legislation. The country implemented a widely criticised counter-terrorism law in 2014 and this was replaced by a penal law for crimes of terrorism and its financing on 1 November 2017. The new legislation was intended to mollify critics, but it has failed to do so.

The 2017 legislation transferred powers from the country's interior ministry to two bodies that report directly to the King, the Public

Prosecution and the Presidency of the State Security. In an analysis of the law, the Swiss-based human rights NGO Alkarama Foundation said that the legislation "lacks legal certainty and can be used to criminalise a wide spectrum of acts falling under the rights to freedom of opinion, expression, peaceful assembly and association as well as the freedom of thought, conscience and religion enshrined in the Universal Declaration of Human Rights."

Human Rights Watch said at the time that it had particular concerns over criminal penalties imposed for portraying the King or Crown Prince "in a manner that brings religion or justice into disrepute" and which also criminalised a wide range of peaceful acts that bear no relation to terrorism.

According to Lina al-Hathloul, head of monitoring and advocacy at Saudi-focused human rights organisation ALQST, the vagueness of the laws means anything could be seen as a form of dissent.

She told Index: "People get 30 to 40-year sentences for tweets or snapchats that are deemed political statements when it's not even dissent. I've seen people get harsh sentences for tweeting and complaining about unemployment, for example.

"People can get arrested without a warrant, and forcibly disappeared. Investigations can be brutal and violent, and in some regions, people are tortured for false confessions. This is especially true of the Shia minority," said al-Hathloul. "Everything is a red line, and everything can lead you to prison. We're getting to a point where absolutely everybody is scared."

The sentences given to women human rights defenders and their supporters are among some of the most egregious [see box on p.19].

In December 2021, the United States Commission on International Religious Freedom said in a report (see **tinyurl. com/saudiCIRF**), "The SCC imposes harsher sentences than other Saudi criminal courts for similar offences, →

ABOVE: Victims of the regime (left-to-right) Youssef al-Manasef; Shadly Ahmad Mahmoud Abou Taqiqa al-Huwaiti; Jalal al-Labad; Ibrahim Salih Ahmad Abou Khalil al-Huwaiti; Salma al-Shehab

→ routinely denies defendants access to legal counsel, and delays issuing judicial decisions. The court's convictions are sometimes based on confessions obtained through torture."

Testimonies seen by Index corroborate these claims of torture.

Following arrests between 2014 and 2021 several people have been subject to severe physical and psychological torture, including beatings, electrocution and death threats. Some were hospitalised as a result and have since developed health complications. However, the Saudi courts have failed to investigate their complaints regarding torture and have instead allowed their coerced confessions to be used as evidence.

Jalal al-Labad was arrested by the authorities from his family's home in al Awamiyah in relation to his participation in protests against the state's treatment of Shia citizens in al-Qatif. Al Labad appeared before the SCC in 2019 and was charged with "participating in demonstrations" and "attending funerals of victims shot by government forces". He was aged 15 at the time of some of his alleged crimes.

He was denied the opportunity of presenting evidence to SCC judges, in the form of recordings from the interrogation rooms, which demonstrated that he had been placed under duress while being interviewed. In a statement to the SCC judges his lawyer said, "Brutally beating the accused with pipes and shoes and cables, banging his head on the table until he passed out, electrocuting him and threatening him with certain death if he did not attest his confession, invalidates the investigation process."

In July 2022, al Labad was sentenced to death, a sentence upheld by the appeals court in October of that year.

Al Labad's case is not an isolated incident. Youssef al-Manasef, who is also facing the death sentence for alleged crimes committed while he was a minor, asserts: "Everything I said was at the dictation of the investigation team and under torture."

Many others have shared similar stories and said they have been denied access to legal representation and have not been able to contact their families.

Al-Hathloul said: "If Saudi Arabia was truly comfortable with its human rights situation, it would allow access to human rights monitors, which it doesn't." Instead, Saudi Arabia is spending oil dollars in an effort to make the problem go away, using the money to host and buy into high-profile sporting events and to fund the world's biggest infrastructure project.

In 2022, Saudi Arabia made a whopping $326 billion from exporting crude oil and the state oil company,

Saudi Aramco, made profits of $161 billion, continuing its streak as one the most profitable companies in the world. The country's sovereign wealth fund, the Public Investment Fund (PIF), manages $700 billion of the country's money. That money is now being spent to launder the country's reputation.

The eagerness of Saudi authorities to be involved in large scale single sporting events is clear for all to see. In the last two years, the Saudi city of Jeddah hosted the country's first Formula One race, and more recently a fight involving heavyweight boxer Anthony Joshua. The brother of Mustafa al Khayat, a human rights defender killed in a mass execution by the Saudi state last year, wrote to Joshua beforehand urging him to speak out against the country's human rights abuses.

This year the Saudi state's involvement in international sport has progressed from hosting one-off events to investing in and buying some of the most iconic sports organisations and athletes in the world. Cristiano Ronaldo completed a move to the Saudi Pro League side Al Nassr, with a reported €200 million ($220 million) annual salary, the highest of any footballer ever. The club is owned by the Public Investment Fund, which also signalled its interest in football with the purchase of Premier League club Newcastle in 2021. Another Public Investment Fund-owned side, Saudi Pro League team Al Hilal bid a world record €300 million ($329 million) for Paris Saint-Germain's French superstar Kylian Mbappe in July 2023. The player rejected it. Many other big players such as Karim Benzema,

≡ Everything is a red line, and everything can lead you to prison

N'Golo Kante and Jordan Henderson have been lured to Saudi Arabia though. Allan Saint-Maximin, Ruben Neves and Fabinho have also moved from the English Premier League. These three are under the age of 30 and are in the prime of their careers. Their transfers have served to confound the view that the Saudi Pro League is a place where older players are put out to pasture.

It's in the game of golf, not football, where the Saudi authorities have had the most influence. LIV Golf is a Saudi-backed professional golf tour, set up as a rival to the established North American-based PGA tour. LIV has a prize fund of more than $400 million and the organisers have enticed players like

Dustin Johnson, Sergio Garcia and Ian Poulter with offers of enormous sums to participate. After LIV was established, a civil war engulfed golf, with the PGA tour warning its own members it would sanction any golfer who signed up for lucrative LIV Golf events. Faced with Saudi's impossibly deep pockets and a series of lawsuits between the two organisations, a merger between the tours was agreed in June 2023.

Human Rights Watch says the merger has allowed the Saudi government to "sportswash its egregious human rights record" and will largely control professional golf.

Adam Crafton, a football journalist for the Athletic, was hesitant to use the term "sportswashing" over Saudi Arabia's investments in sport. Speaking to Index, he said: "There is a genuine attempt from the Saudi state to diversify

the economy and move it away from oil and gas. It's another sector for them to invest in.

"However, certainly one of the consequences of their huge move into sports has been to help their trajectory from borderline pariah state after the Jamal al Khashoggi killing to regaining a foothold with the West again.

"There are lots of different layers to this. At the same time the real issues are questions about human rights, freedoms and civil liberties. They're all the same conversation."

Saudi Arabia is not just investing in sporting crown jewels to distract attention from its shocking human rights record. No project symbolises the country's efforts to be seen as a good global citizen more than the vast Neom megacity project, which is being planned and built in the country's north-west. →

BELOW: Satellite imagery of Neom showing the site isn't as barren as made out

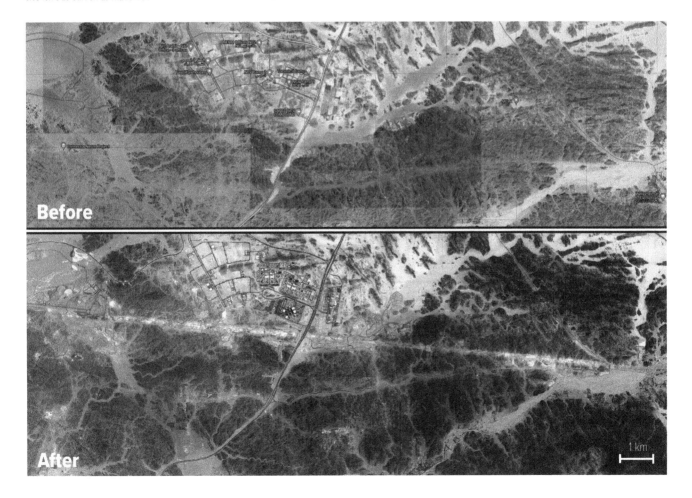

Before

After

1 km

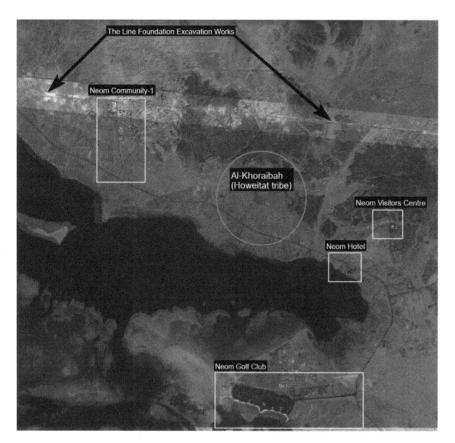

The Line Foundation Excavation Works

Neom Community-1

Al-Khoraibah
(Howeitat tribe)

Neom Visitors Centre

Neom Hotel

Neom Golf Club

LEFT: People living on the land where Neom is being built have been forcibly removed

→ Neom measures 36,500 square kilometres, roughly the size of Belgium. Its developers call it a "home for people who dream big", a "hub for innovation" and "an entirely new model for sustainable living".

Neom includes a port city called Oxagon that aims to attract the 13% of the world's trade that passes through the Suez Canal, a ski resort called Trojena and a 170-kilometre long, 500-metre high and 200-metre wide city called The Line with no cars or roads and nine million residents.

It is set to be the world's most expensive infrastructure project, worth at least $500 billion and potentially double that. This huge investment represents a massive payday for many of the world's biggest firms, including architects, construction companies, management consultants, hotel companies and engineers.

With such a high-profile project attracting attention from around the world, the Saudi regime has been keen to silence domestic critics. According to the UN, since January 2020 the Saudi authorities have reportedly carried out a series of actions to evict members of the Howeitat tribe from their homes and traditional lands in three villages, Al Khuraiba, Sharma and Gayal, to allow the project to proceed. The UN says despite promises that residents would be involved in the process and receive fair compensation, this appears not to have happened. Six Howeitat tribe members who objected to the development have been arrested and tried.

The MENA Rights Group says three of the six were arrested at a family farm by agents under the control of the Saudi Presidency of State Security but who did not have arrest warrants. The group says that after his arrest Shadli Ahmad Mahmoud Abou Taqiqa-al Huwaiti was subject to beatings, electrocutions and forced to stand on one leg in the sun all day at al Tarrfiyyah prison in al Qasim in order to get him to confess that he had established a terrorist cell.

On 5 August 2022 Shadli, along with Ibrahim Salih Ahmad Abou Khalil al-Huwaiti and Atallah Moussa Mohammed al-Huwaiti, were reportedly sentenced to death by the SCC while three others, Abdelnasser Ahmad Mahmoud Abou Taqiqa al-Huwaiti, Mahmoud Ahmad Mahmoud Abou Taqiqa al-Huwaiti and Abdullah Dakhilallah al-Huwaiti, were handed sentences ranging from 27 to 50 years.

Following the sentencing, a group of UN experts, including Special Rapporteur on Freedom of Opinion and Expression Irene Khan, issued a statement:

"Despite being charged with terrorism, they were reportedly arrested for resisting forced evictions in the name of the Neom project and the construction of a 170 kilometre linear city called The Line."

The statement (see **tinyurl.com/ saudiOHCHR**) indicated that the UN experts had contacted the government, the Saudi Public Investment Fund and the NEOM company in addition to 18 foreign companies involved in the project. One of those companies is Britain's InterContinental Hotels Group.

The company has recently announced that one of its properties will open at the Neom megaproject in 2026.

Haitham Mattar, managing director, India, Middle East & Africa, for IHG, said in a press release: "We are delighted to announce our first IHG hotel in the

 Everything I said was at the dictation of the investigation team and under torture

exciting and rapidly developing region of NEOM...As our presence in the market continues to grow, we are committed to supporting the goals of Saudi Vision 2030 by offering exceptional hospitality experiences to leisure and business travellers visiting the country."

Saudi Vision 2030 is an MBS-inspired project that uses Saudi's "investment power to create a more diverse and sustainable economy".

Index asked IHG for a comment about investing in the country with its chequered human rights record, but it did not respond before publication.

Saudi Arabia's efforts are clearly working. In 2022, the Joe Biden administration said that MBS should enjoy sovereign immunity over the Khashoggi case. The UK has also now invited MBS on an official visit this autumn; the government is keen to secure a free trade deal with the Gulf Cooperation Council, of which Saudi is a leading member.

In its 2022 annual report on human rights in Saudi Arabia, Sanad, which aims to alleviate the suffering of arbitrarily detained individuals in Saudi Arabia, highlighted how countries are turning a blind eye to the problem. Sanad's chair Saeed al Ghamdi said: "Crown Prince Mohammed bin Salman is intent in crushing any form of dissent in the most brutal of fashions, all with the apparent unwillingness or inability of the international community to expose the human rights violations carried out in his name."

Sanad highlighted the visit of former British Prime Minister Boris Johnson to the country. On the day of his visit on 12 March 2022, Saudi Arabia carried out "the largest mass execution in the country's history" when "81 citizens were executed on charges relating to freedom of opinion and expression".

Duaa Dhainy, researcher and advocacy associate at the European Saudi Organization for Human Rights, believes Saudi Arabia has taken advantage of global political

Women's rights and the SCC

THE SENTENCES HANDED down by the SCC to women's rights defenders and their supporters are particularly harsh. In the past few years, huge numbers of people have been tried by the Specialised Criminal Court in cases that relate to freedom of expression, such as calling for an end to Saudi's male guardianship system or criticising Saudi Arabia's rulers on social media.

Nourah bint Saeed al Qahtani was sentenced to 45 years in prison for "violating public order by using social media" under Counter-Terrorism Law and Anti-Cyber Crime Law. Among her "crimes" were "breaking the social fabric in the Kingdom" by criticising Saudi rulers, "violating the public order by using social media" and "producing and storing of materials impinging on public order and religious values".

On 15 January 2021, Saudi national Salma al Shehab, who was a PhD student at the University of Leeds in the UK at the time, was arrested after going to Saudi Arabia to spend the holiday with her family. She was questioned for almost a year before being charged under various parts of the country's counter-terrorism law and the anti-cybercrime law for "supporting those seeking to disrupt public order, undermining the safety of the general public and stability of the state, and publishing false and tendentious rumours on Twitter".

Al Shehab was initially handed a six-year sentence but on appeal this was increased to 34 years, including a discretionary five years added by the judge. She was also slapped with a travel ban for a further 34 years following her sentence. After a

retrial in January 2023, the sentence was reduced to 27 years. During the retrial, the presiding judge denied al Shehab the right to speak in her defence.

The Working Group on Arbitrary Detention of the Human Rights Council has challenged the Saudi government over the cases of al Qahtani and al Shehab. The Saudi government was given a right to reply. It said: "The crimes committed by Ms al Shehab and Ms al Qahtani are unrelated to freedom of expression as they have been convicted of terrorism-related offences...The Government reiterates that Ms al Shehab and Ms al Qahtani were arrested on charges of terrorism, therefore, their arrests had nothing to do with their political opinions, gender or religion. ...The Government submits that Ms al Shehab and Ms al Qahtani have been treated in a manner that preserves their dignity and protects their rights. Both individuals have enjoyed the right to regular visits and communications. Ms al Shehab has not been subjected to torture or ill-treatment."

Analysing the cases, the working group concluded (see **tinyurl.com/saudiHRC**) that the jailing of Salma al Shehab and Nourah bin Saeed al Qahtani were in contravention of various articles of the Universal Declaration of Human Rights and that they should be released immediately. The working group called on the Saudi government to "revise its laws, particularly the anti-terrorism law, to meet the requirements of due process and a fair trial, in conformity with the findings in the present opinion and with its obligations under international law".

and economic struggles. Dhainy said: "There was a way to lift the diplomatic blockade that lasted for a period after the killing of Khashoggi. They just bought the silence of countries."

ALQST's al-Hathloul says the primary intention of the Saudi investments is to change the way people think about what happens in Saudi Arabia.

She said: "They're not saying that by investing in sports people will forget about Khashoggi. However, it leads to

people forgetting about human rights. So in that sense, it is working. It rebrands the image of Saudi Arabia.

"For young people, when they now think of Saudi Arabia they may just think of Ronaldo instead of the abuse of women's and civil rights." ✖

Francis Clarke is editorial assistant and Mark Frary is associate editor at Index

52(03):12/17|DOI:10.1177/03064220231201268

Pinochet's ghost still haunts

Fifty years after Augusto Pinochet's bloody coup in Chile, the nation continues to grapple with the demons he unleashed. **JUAN CARLOS RAMÍREZ FIGUEROA** reports

ONE HUNDRED AND nineteen silhouettes stand in the centre of Santiago. But only 400 people have come out in the pouring rain to commemorate the people these figures represent.

The silhouettes in the capital of Chile were created by artist José Rodríguez in 2005 and they represent the victims of Operation Colombo, when Augusto Pinochet's regime executed political opponents (119 documented at the time). The event gave rise to the famous headline in evening newspaper La Segunda, "Exterminated like rats".

Half a century after the 1973 coup that overthrew the democratic government of Salvador Allende, 36% of Chileans believe that the military "were right" in executing those involved

in the coup, according to a Mori opinion poll – Chile In the Shadow of Pinochet – carried out this year. That is 10 percentage points higher than it was in 2013. Also this year, Luis Silva, constitutional adviser to the far-right Republican Party, stated in an interview that he felt "admiration" for the general and saw him as a "statesman" capable of "rebuilding a shattered state".

Silva's party won the majority in the recent plebiscite, where constitutional advisers were elected to draft a new constitution, replacing the one imposed by Pinochet in 1980. This was after the rejection of the first attempt at a new constitution, led by left-wing parties, which emerged as a political solution to the crisis caused by the Social Outbreak of October 2019, when over

ABOVE: Augusto Pinochet, when he was dictator of Chile and commander-in-chief of the Chilean army, 1989

one million people protested against the government of Sebastián Piñera. More than 300 people were shot in the eye with police pellet guns during the months-long protests, which formed the country's biggest crisis since its return to democracy.

The proposed constitution was rejected last year in what was a significant defeat for the government of the progressive president Gabriel Boric, who – as a congressman – had reached an agreement with Piñera over it.

Boric responded to Silva's comments on Pinochet on social media, stating: "Augusto Pinochet was a dictator, essentially anti-democratic, whose government killed, tortured, exiled and made disappear those who thought differently. He was also corrupt and a thief. Cowardly to the end, he did everything in his power to evade justice."

During a visit to Europe in July, Boric awarded a recognition medal to Baltasar Garzón, the Spanish judge who issued the arrest warrant against Pinochet while he was visiting London in 1998 on charges of genocide, international terrorism, forced disappearances and torture, among others. The right-wing strongly criticised this decoration. Superficially they said they opposed it because Garzón had later participated in an international lawsuit by Bolivia against Chile. But the real reason may be that he was the man who broke one of the agreements of the return to democracy: to leave the general in peace.

Even though at least 3,000 were executed or disappeared when Pinochet was in power, tens of thousands were tortured and an estimated 200,000 fled the country, Pinochetism has never disappeared from Chile. On the flipside, some look back at his dictatorship in a positive light. The historian Cristina Moyano Barahona believes there is a reason for this, if ill-founded. Moyano cites what Steve J Stern pointed out in Remembering Pinochet's Chile, that the general embodied the idea of saving the country from the political, moral and economic debacle it was facing.

"This frame of reference gives meaning not only to the critical view of Allende's government but also to certain social sectors that politicised themselves outside of the elites. This has been inherited across generations, and it should not surprise us. Perhaps it has lost some of its hegemony, but we cannot forget that in 1988, when 'No' won, there was still 43% of the population that wanted Pinochet to continue ruling," said Barahona.

In this context, Barahona added, there is still support for Pinochet in the Republican Party, including from

Chile never had prohibition of the cult of certain images linked to the dictatorship, as happened in Germany with Hitler

the likes of Silva; former presidential candidate José Antonio Kast (who won the first round of voting in the last presidential election before losing to Boric in the run-off); and the president of the Constitutional Council, Beatriz Hevia, who won't comment on the dictatorship because "I was born in 1992 and referring to events I did not live and do not know in detail, beyond what one can know and learn, makes no sense".

Barahona also pointed out: "Chile never had prohibition of the cult of certain images linked to the dictatorship, as happened in Germany with Hitler. This allows Pinochet to still be present and used within an ethical relativism where, for many, it does not matter that people were killed, as long as there was a supposed order or wellbeing."

The photographer Marcelo Montealegre, renowned for his portraits and activism in documenting Chilean exiles and himself one of Pinochet's victims, is disheartened by the continued support of Pinochet.

"It seems desolating to me," he said.

"The problem, I believe, is that the 60% opposed to Pinochetism are not a coherent or united force. The right has always known how to support candidates from different backgrounds if they perceive that their interests are less threatened than [they are by] the alternatives."

Regarding the vindication of the dictatorship, Montealegre believes it is a natural phenomenon. He said that as right-wing groups regain ground, they will use the public stage more frequently. And he highlighted problems that occurred during the transition.

"Pinochet himself warned that he would not accept accusations or actions

against 'his own'," he said. "This, in my opinion, is the most critical point of the return to democracy. In Uruguay, there was a plebiscite, and voters decided to turn the page. In Argentina, the military were tried, and many ended up in jail. In Chile, neither of these has happened, despite the evidence that has been collected over the decades."

Pinochet was in power until 1990, two years after losing a plebiscite vote to extend his rule in Chile by eight years. But even though he was eventually voted out, he still occupied key positions within Chile's political structure. Pablo Matus, an academic from the Pontifical Catholic University of Chile, believes that's one of the reasons his allure remains. Matus said that "what distinguishes the Chilean transition is that the dictatorship's leaders remained in power or retained influence": José Toribio Merino left the navy shortly before the change of government, but his influence was evident in the admirals ➔

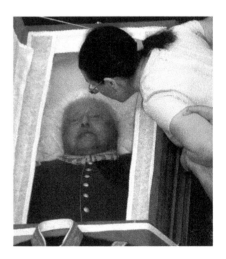

ABOVE: A supporter of Pinochet kisses his coffin as he lies in state at the Military Academy in Santiago, Chile, December 2006

LEFT: People bid farewell to Luisa Toledo, mother of two boys who were murdered by police during Pinochet's dictatorship. Toledo dedicated her life to justice for the victims of Pinochet

→ who succeeded him; Fernando Matthei was commander-in-chief of the air force until 1991; Rodolfo Stange was head of the police force until 1995; and Pinochet himself was commander-in-chief of the army until 1998.

"That's why during [Patricio] Aylwin's government, there was always a fear of a new coup," said Matus.

In fact, during the dictatorship, the entire Supreme Court was installed, and it continued to function during Aylwin's early years of rule. It was naive to believe that the justice system would prosecute the leaders of the military junta.

"Another thing is the political and moral judgment about Pinochet – for example, denying his involvement in, and even knowledge of, human rights violations [and] indirectly implicating all his subordinates," added Matus. "In this sense, Chile lacked someone who recognised, on behalf of the armed forces, the tremendous error committed, as Martín Balza did in Argentina."

Sociologist Eugenio Tironi, who as a member of the Popular Unitary Action Movement was part of the resistance to the dictatorship abroad, was instrumental in the "socialist renewal" and played a key role in the Chilean transition to democracy. He said: "There is more commotion, interest and public debate than in previous anniversaries, but there is a noticeable change: the greater prominence of those who perpetrated, supported and justified the coup and the dictatorship. The old taboos have been lost."

He said another change was the reappearance of a rift among the opponents of the dictatorship, some of whom were trying to control how the anniversary was honoured. Indeed Patricio Fernández, the writer and founder of The Clinic newspaper – which was founded soon after Pinochet was arrested at The London Clinic in 1998 (he was later released) – had to resign from his position as co-ordinator of the 50th-anniversary events after he gave an interview in which he focused more on the future than on explicitly condemning the attack on La Moneda,

the presidential seat, and the coup.

This speaks of a greater fear, namely that in line with other countries around the world, specific parts of Chile are moving more towards shutting down conversations.

"In this sense, Chile seems to be part of a global trend more prone to authoritarianism. This is also aided by the radical position of some [on the] left wing who, by denying any self-criticism of their own past behaviour, justify the rupture of dialogue from the revisionist currents," said Tironi.

He doesn't believe, though, that there has been a lack of social judgment against those responsible for the horrors of the dictatorship. He said: "There are few countries in the world that have made as much progress in truth and justice in human rights matters after a dictatorship. There are gaps, no doubt, such as not knowing the fate of thousands of detainees who disappeared, but the achievements are undeniable, thanks in part to international justice."

Back at the commemoration in Santiago, testimonies are heard from mothers who have been searching for information about their missing children since 1973, and from people such as 71-year-old Mario Aguilera, who says they were there to continue to highlight that "many are still missing".

But Barahona said: "If you had asked me a decade ago what the 50th anniversary of the coup would be like, I would have said without hesitation that there would be a consolidation of democratic culture and human rights. Today, I believe that those of us who thought that were completely wrong." ✖

Juan Carlos Ramírez Figueroa is a journalist based in Santiago

52(03):18/20|DOI:10.1177/03064220231201269

 Testimonies are heard from mothers who have been searching for information about their missing children since 1973

CREDIT: Claudio Abarca Sandoval/NurPhoto/Alamy

The dissident lives on

ABOVE: Imprisoned journalist and public figure Vladimir Kara-Murza during a court session this July in Moscow

When the Soviet Union collapsed people said the dissident would die.
MARTIN BRIGHT explores how history has proven otherwise

TO ADAPT THE Mark Twain quote, the death of the dissident has been greatly exaggerated. It has even been announced on more than one occasion in the pages of Index on Censorship. In the very first issue of the magazine in 1972, editor Michael Scammell said a definite need existed for Index to publicise the treatment and work of dissidents, "but only time will tell whether the need is temporary or permanent". It has remained a sad necessity for more than 50 years, but it didn't always seem that way.

In 1987, as glasnost ushered in a new era for writers, artists and intellectuals in the Soviet Union, Scammel's successor George Theiner, himself a Czech dissident, wrote of his

hopes for the new age of freedom for the USSR. "While we still devote a good many pages to the fate of Soviet writers and other intellectuals, this is largely due to the consequences of glasnost, which has cleared the way for a much franker discussion and for criticism of Soviet conditions of a kind that was unthinkable only a short time ago," he said. Tragically, he never lived to see his hopes come to pass, dying just a year later, before the fall of the Berlin Wall.

In February 1990, Václav Havel, who had been transformed from political prisoner to president of Czechoslovakia, wrote for Index: "It looks as if we've come to the end of a period which, for the sake of argument and brevity, might be described as 'classic dissidence', even though it is an ugly and imprecise label." These were heady times in Eastern Europe and those who wrote for Index can be forgiven for thinking a better world was possible. After the collapse of communism, the countries of the former Soviet bloc were swept along in a market-driven wave of →

 In its way, the emergence of Vladimir Putin has been every bit as bewildering as the fall of communism

The tension between conspiracy and openness remains at the heart of the debate over dissident tactics

→ democratic optimism. Before the outbreak of conflict in the Balkans, German reunification and EU expansion suggested a new dawn really had arrived.

Writing in the same February 1990 edition, poet and Index founder Stephen Spender remembered a conversation with his friend, the philosopher Isaiah Berlin, from the previous year when both men turned 80. "The one thing I wished to live to see was the collapse of the dictatorships in the Soviet Union and eastern Europe. He agreed but said alas this would not happen in our lifetimes." Spender's next paragraph is haunting in the context of Russia today. "Well, now it has happened, and the results are completely bewildering. We can certainly

hope that in that part of the world... we shall have far less need to be concerned with prisoners of conscience."

He can be forgiven for not predicting that three decades later, dissidents would still face persecution in Russia. He could not have foreseen the fates of Alexey Navalny and Vladimir Kara-Murza, let alone those of Anna Politkovskaya and Alexander Litvinenko. In its way, the emergence of Vladimir Putin has been every bit as bewildering as the fall of communism.

It is easy to understand Havel's desire to announce the demise of what he described as "classic dissidence" in 1990, when he was entering the presidential castle in Prague as the

head of the newly independent and democratic Czech state. But this was not the first time Index had been used to write the obituary of the dissident.

At the end of the 1970s an intense row broke out in the pages of this magazine between two very distinct tendencies in the Soviet opposition movement. On one side stood a new breed of Soviet human rights activist, keen to expose the abuses of the Soviet regime and take up the causes of individual dissidents. Best known among them was Anatoly Shcharansky, who (as Natan Sharansky) went on to become a prominent Israeli politician. On the other side stood the socialist dissident historian Roy Medvedev and his twin brother Zhores, a prominent scientist. The Medvedev brothers were among the most famous Soviet opposition figures in the West, only really rivalled at the time by the novelist Alexander Solzhenitsyn.

In September 1978, Roy Medvedev published an open letter criticising fellow dissident Alexander Ginzburg after he was arrested and put on trial for anti-Soviet activities. Ginzburg managed the Russian Social Fund, which helped political prisoners and their families. Medvedev felt Ginzburg had been careless in the way he compiled card indexes of thousands of names and addresses of dissidents and their supporters. These could then be used to target those identified by the authorities.

Writing in Index in February 1979, Medvedev grandly announced that "by the second half of the sixties... the dissident movement was already beginning to decline, and this trend has continued into the seventies."

Medvedev was a fierce critic of the abuses of the Communist regime, but he did not support the human rights approach to opposition activity, which he saw as a distraction from the wider struggle for Soviet reform and the

LEFT: A man stops in front of a film poster in Moscow, April 1976

improvement of the living conditions for millions of ordinary Soviet citizens. He even likened this approach to The People's Will, the revolutionary terrorists of the Tsarist era. "Just as the members of Narodnaya Volya (The People's Will) in their day were drawn into terror, into acts of vengeance for vengeance's sake, so many dissidents have gradually reduced the human rights struggle to a struggle, however noble, for the release of their friends, for the right to go abroad, for the easing of labour camp regimes and so forth."

Medvedev's letter sparked a furious response. Elena Bonner, the wife of Nobel Peace Prize laureate Andrei Sakharov, likened Medvedev's criticisms to those made by the KGB in the Russian media. In a full-throated response to Medvedev in the March 1979 edition of Index, the Ukrainian novelist Georgi Vladimov argued that dissidents were right to be open and candid in their activities in contrast to the secretive methods of the regime. In a direct challenge to Medvedev's characterisation of the human rights movement, Vladimov wrote: "An underground terrorist group is at work, the only difference being that it is not hounded by this government – it is the government".

Barbara Martin, author of Roy and Zhores Medvedev: Loyal Dissent in the Soviet Union, which was published this July, told Index that Medvedev's position was informed by the research he had done into the history of communism. This brought him into contact with revolutionaries from the Tsarist era.

"Medvedev had interacted a lot with old Bolsheviks, and they had taught him the rules of conspiracy, which is this whole heritage of the revolutionary

who had to hide from the Tsarist regime. And Medvedev is someone who was extremely skilled with these things. That's also one of the keys to his survival. He used these techniques a lot and, for him, it was really a shame that Ginzburg had so little of these skills.

"Basically, the human rights movement had the opposite position: for them the keyword was *glasnost*, openness. They wanted to make everything public. And this implied that they could be arrested much more easily."

Martin said the Medvedev-Vladimov debate has interesting contemporary echoes. Navalny faced similar criticism of negligence in 2021 when emails of supporters who had signed up to protests found their way online. "This is very much the same kind of thing that Medvedev was accusing Ginzburg of. These letters raised a huge reaction from the dissident movement. They were saying 'you cannot accuse a man who's in prison' and Vladimov was also defending this position of openness saying 'this is the way we do it in this movement and we don't want this heritage of conspiracy'."

The tension between conspiracy and openness remains at the heart of the debate over dissident tactics. Other features of the debate from the 1970s are also familiar, such as whether it is best to choose exile or to raise the alarm from within, a tactic which has become an increasingly dangerous pursuit in Putin's Russia.

In April 1979 Alexander Ginzburg was stripped of his Soviet citizenship and expelled to the USA as part of a prisoner exchange. It is instructive to compare the subsequent careers of the two writers who crossed swords in Index over his arrest. Vladimov,

ABOVE: Dissident brothers Roy Medvedev (L) and Zhores Medvedev

who headed the Moscow branch of Amnesty International at the time of the controversy, continued to write novels and plays that were deeply critical of the Soviet military and the KGB. In 1983 he emigrated to West Germany. His novel about Kyiv during World War II, the General and His Army, won the Russian Booker Prize in 1994. Vladimov's Russian citizenship was restored in 2000 and when he died in 2003 his Guardian obituary read: "His life was one of constant vicissitudes, but his authority and fortitude remained firm to the end."

Medvedev remained in the Soviet Union, where he continued to argue for reform from within. In 1989 he rejoined the Communist Party and was elected to the Congress of People's Deputies. After the fall of the regime, he helped found the new Socialist Workers' Party. Still writing at the age of 97, Medvedev is now a cheerleading biographer of Putin. The book that brought him fame as a dissident in 1972 was called Let History Judge, which examined the legacy of Stalin. Now history will judge him. ✖

Martin Bright is Index editor-at-large

52(03):21/23|DOI:10.1177/03064220231201294

Medvedev felt Ginzburg had been careless in the way he compiled indexes of thousands of dissidents

No place to hide

Gone are the days when distance meant safety. Now autocrats are using digital tools to persecute dissidents no matter where they are in the world, writes **NIK WILLIAMS**

"YOU HAVE NO sovereignty where we gather. We have no elected government, nor are we likely to have one, so I address you with no greater authority than that with which liberty itself always speaks." On 8 February 1996 in Davos, Switzerland, the activist John Perry Barlow committed the manifesto of cyber-utopianism to paper in A Declaration of the Independence of Cyberspace. Issued as a statement of intent, the declaration positions emergent internet-enabled networks as a space beyond established concepts of territoriality and state control. Nearly three decades later, it reads like a prediction of a future that never came to pass.

Authoritarianism is an exploration in outcome thinking. Autocrats seek a space where their power is absolute and will use any tactic they can to arrive at that objective. In this way, repression has expanded to match the opening-up of online spaces. Despots across the globe have realised that if the internet is everywhere, their repression can follow, crossing borders effortlessly. The US sociologist Dana Moss coined a term to describe the ways authoritarian regimes respond to opposition from outside their borders: transnational repression.

Yana Gorokhovskaia, research director at the human rights organisation Freedom House, painted a picture to me of a modern world tailor-made for transnational repression because there are more ways to communicate and there is more migration. According to Gorokhovskaia, the proliferation of digital communication tools is a double-edged sword. "On the one hand

that makes people's voices in exile that much more influential because they are able to sit in the USA and talk to the Iranians, or someone in Central Asia, but it also provides governments with the opportunity to find them and track them."

Before the advent of digital technologies, the targeting of dissidents in other states was a high risk and expensive exercise, which meant it was usually reserved for only the most high-value targets. However, as digital tools have become cheaper and more prevalent, the costs have plummeted. In an article published from this May in the European Journal of International Security, researchers Marcus Michaelsen and Johannes Thumfart highlight the economies at play: "Digital threats against exiled opponents reduce the costs of extraterritorial political control. They no longer need to send agents abroad to spy on and intimidate critics in the diaspora. With minimal costs and risk of consequences, a successful hacking attack against a single activist in the diaspora can expose a trove of confidential communications and unravel entire networks".

Breaching the Firewall
"I can tell you very clear, we had nothing to do with this horrible murder". These are the words of Shalev Hulio, the former chief executive of NSO

Group, an Israeli private surveillance company that was behind the Pegasus spyware tool, when he spoke to the CBS documentary show 60 Minutes in March 2019. He was referring to the gruesome murder of journalist Jamal Khashoggi in the Saudi consulate in Turkey in October 2018, which US intelligence agencies concluded in a declassified report from 2021 was approved of by Saudi crown prince Mohammed bin Salman. Through the Pegasus Project, led by journalists' network Forbidden Stories and an international consortium of media organisations, it was discovered that numerous contacts of Khashoggi had been targeted for surveillance and that Pegasus spyware was used.

NSO Group states that it only sells to vetted countries "for the sole purpose of saving lives through preventing crime and terror acts", and yet reports of Pegasus infections have spanned the globe, with Forbidden Stories claiming that "evidence of Pegasus attacks has been found in the phones of more than 420 individuals of over 30 nationalities across four continents, including more than 120 journalists and more than 130 human rights activists, political activists and lawyers." The increased availability of commercial spyware means "countries that are incredibly resource rich, like China, are able to use this technology but also countries we tend to think of as weaker authoritarian powers like Uzbekistan or Turkmenistan are also able to buy off-the-shelf spyware and use it against people," said Gorokhovskaia.

Faustin Rukundo is a Rwandan exile now living in Leeds in the UK. As a member of the opposition movement – the Rwanda National Congress – he decided to flee Rwanda as he "wanted to live, be free, have a life that is not

Despots across the globe have realised that if the internet is everywhere, their repression can follow

ABOVE: Activists and journalists hold a vigil outside the Saudi Arabian embassy in Dublin, Republic of Ireland for murdered journalist Jamal Khashoggi, 2018

controlled". Like many members of diaspora communities, WhatsApp was vital for keeping in touch. He told me that WhatsApp "looked to be one of the most secure ways of communicating and it was cheap as well." However, in April 2019, Rukundo noticed inexplicable things happening on his phone. "You could see that some files are going missing. You will see silly things happening on your screen." And then the phone calls started. In his words, "I got some missed calls coming from Scandinavian countries and then some other missed calls that I could not even trace because I wouldn't even see them." Rukundo said subsequent missed calls would again vanish before he could return the call and if he was able to call back the calls would not connect. It was around this time that he was contacted by Citizen Lab who analysed his devices and discovered that he had been infected with Pegasus.

Rukundo started to notice something about the files that went missing too. Two years earlier, in 2017, Rukundo's pregnant wife Violette Uwamahoro was held in Rwanda after returning for a family funeral. She was charged with spreading state secrets but, according to the BBC, "a judge said there was no evidence to warrant the detention of the expectant mother and released her on bail." She returned to the UK. However, one of the files that disappeared, Rukundo claims, related to communications he had had with the British government and his local MP, who continued to ask him questions ➔

CREDIT: Eddie Gerald/Alamy

→ about why she was arrested. "They want to know who I speak to especially here in the UK and not necessarily people from Rwanda but UK officials because they were so much interested in how I speak to my MP," he told Index.

Rwanda has publicly stated that it "does not use this software system … and does not possess this technical capability in any form." However, according to the Organized Crime and Corruption Reporting Project (OCCRP), as part of the Pegasus Project, "more

than 3,500 Rwandan phone numbers appeared on the leaked Pegasus list, indicating that they were potential targets of the software." Rwanda said the reporting was "part of an ongoing campaign to cause tensions between Rwanda and other countries, and to sow disinformation about Rwanda domestically and internationally".

The lack of transparency over Rwanda's capabilities has fostered concern throughout Rwandan civil society. A digital rights activist, who

asked to remain anonymous, told me that "the capacity of state intelligence services in terms of deploying technology against dissidents is known, but we don't know precisely their capacity in terms of technology used, in terms of what is the modus operandi and how long the Rwandan government has been investing in this kind of technology."

They were not optimistic as to whether this information would ever be forthcoming: "You will never know what is going on," they said.

LEFT: Activists call for accountability and increased controls on the international sale of spyware technology in front of the building housing the NSO group, which develops the spyware Pegasus in Herzliya, Israel, in 2021

moving to Canada in August 1989. As soon as she arrived in Canada, she started to speak to Canadian media outlets. That was enough for the attacks to start. Offline threats migrated online in the early 2000s. When researching a book, she claims a virus targeted her computer leading it to crash. "I didn't understand what was happening," she told Index. Alongside a group of other campaigners who were targeted, they contacted the Royal Canadian Mounted Police (RCMP) and sent the suspicious emails to Citizen Lab.

Hers was not an isolated case. In October 2013, Xue organised a conference in Toronto, inviting politicians from Canada, Europe and Japan. According to Xue's retelling, after announcing the opening of the conference on-stage, an attendee approached her to say they'd been sent a photo of her, remarking to her that "you look beautiful". When she asked to see the photo, the attendee showed her a nude photo of herself, or rather of her head and someone else's body. Xue told me that "I didn't give a big reaction, because I know if I reacted, they would use this as the next step. This kind of thing, I think, they feel is very useful [when attacking] a woman." The use of doctored photos continued. Xue later reported a similar attack to the RCMP, who said they could not do anything and recommended Xue sue. How could she though when →

Who benefits?

As quoted by Cicero, the Roman judge Lucius Cassius would often ask "*Cui bono fuisset?*", meaning "who benefits?" NSO Group does not comment on who their client states are and has questioned the veracity of the leaked Pegasus list that underpins the Pegasus Project's reporting. So, while forensic analysis can uncover whether a device has been infected, targets and civil society can usually only draw inferences, based on

the target's identity and background, as to who the client may be.

Sheng Xue was part of the Tiananmen democracy movement before

A successful hacking attack against a single activist in the diaspora can expose a trove of confidential communications and unravel entire networks

→ she didn't know the identity of the perpetrator? Then she was doxed. Her phone numbers were shared online, next to suggestions that she was a sex worker "looking for a boyfriend". She was inundated with calls.

Xue is not a universally liked figure within the pro-democracy movement. For those targeting her, this conflicted status was ripe for exploitation. For example, one activist, Liu Shaofu, claims that "an imposter opened a Twitter account with his name and photo to post criticism of Sheng Xue, including one fake nude photo."

All the while Xue was being spied on, every detail of her life recorded. When Xue later returned to China, she was arrested. Speaking about being detained in Beijing, Xue told me that "they knew everything about me in Canada." An individual, who has remained anonymous, also alleged that his "family was threatened after he was asked to spy on behalf of the CCP after moving in" to Xue's basement.

And yet even after this, definitive proof tying the Chinese state to Xue's abuse is hard to find. In the New York Times, Andy Ellis, the former assistant director of operations for the Canadian Security Intelligence Service, said he believed that the Chinese state was behind the campaign. "I think the Chinese government is trying to sully her reputation to advance their own interests," he wrote. But thinking something is different to knowing.

When asked why Xue thought Beijing was behind the attacks, she answered with a series of legitimate questions: "Who would do all this to one individual for over 30 years? Who has

such resources and capabilities? Who has the incentive to do this? Who is so afraid of my words and actions? Who can use so many people to insult me and attack me?"

Lifting the curtain

Attempting to tie down states as liable for transnational repression is no mean feat. Take this example from 2017. A US citizen who was born in Ethiopia, named in court under the pseudonym Kidane, brought legal action against Ethiopia, alleging that they were behind a spyware attack against him while living in the USA. But the DC Circuit ruled that "it is a transnational tort over which we lack subject matter jurisdiction." In the words of Electronic Frontier Foundation, which acted for Kidane, "because the Ethiopian government hatched its plan in Ethiopia and its agents launched the attack that occurred in Maryland from outside the US, a law called the Foreign Sovereign Immunities Act (FSIA) prevented US courts from even hearing the case."

Ghanem al Masarir is a Saudi satirist now based in London. Around the time of the Arab uprising, he used a range of social media platforms to express his support for the pro-democracy movements. As a result of his online activity, al Masarir claims his accounts on Youtube, Facebook and Twitter were taken down multiple times. He also says his personal website was hacked, and quickly – just 20 minutes after it went live. Al Masarir claims it was hacked to include a picture of King Salman. Speaking to him, he was unequivocal as to who he believed was behind the takedowns and online attacks: the Saudi authorities. In his words "they don't

want to hear your voice … They want to destroy your life, as simple as that".

The online attacks were mirrored in real life. According to al Masarir in August 2018, for example, when he was out in London with a friend he was followed and verbally harassed by two men. This was followed by a physical assault, during which the attackers called him "a slave of Qatar". When he was sitting in the ambulance afterwards, another unknown individual approached al Masarir and identified himself as a Saudi businessman who imported rice into the UK. He turned to al-Masarir's acquaintance and said, "Don't associate yourself with this son of a bitch!" He then warned him that "the police will not come for Ghanem, we are in charge here, we run the police and they will not come."

Al Masarir is now suing the state of Saudi Arabia. In the words of his lawyers at Leigh Day, he "is bringing a claim for the psychological damage resulting from the misuse of private information and harassment in relation to the spyware. He is also bringing a claim relating to a physical attack he suffered on 31 August 2018 outside Harrods which he believes was directed by the Saudi regime."

In 2022, the British High Court ruled that Saudi Arabia does not have immunity under the State Immunity Act 1978, opening the way for a substantive case to be heard. As this case seeks to tie a state to a coordinated set of digital and physical acts of repression, the broader impact cannot be understated.

Stemming the tide

Still, how do we know when a dissident is targeted by a coordinated campaign and not clusters of standalone harassment with no state involvement? How can we overcome the walls of silence from companies such as NSO Group, as well as nation states, to uncover those behind the threats in a manner that enables law enforcement and courts to act?

Following the murder of Khashoggi,

When she asked to see the photo, the attendee showed her a nude photo of herself, or rather of her head and someone else's body

the European Parliament convened a committee on the company, while the USA has moved to prohibit use of commercial spyware, even blacklisting NSO Group in 2021. This treats a symptom but does not address the root problem. NSO Group is only the latest in a long list of companies which could be supporting authoritarian regimes.

The FBI has started to monitor transnational repression, based on situations "[when] foreign governments stalk, intimidate, or assault people in the United States", identifying targets such as political and human rights activists, journalists, political opponents and religious or ethnic minority groups. It also highlights those wanted for crimes of transnational repression, including Sun Qiang, a Chinese citizen who is alleged to have "tasked individuals in the United States to gather information on People's Republic of China (PRC) dissidents by using due-diligence reports, surveillance, GPS trackers and elaborate cover stories."

Other countries have looked to establish new legal devices in response. Sweden has developed an expansive definition of transnational repression in its criminal code and called it refugee espionage or *flyktingspionage*. The Swedish Security Service confirmed to me via a statement that "Russia, China and Iran all conduct intelligence gathering and security-threatening activities against Sweden. Refugee espionage is one of these activities."

This has been tested by the Swedish legal system, as seen in the 2020 attempted assault on Tumso Abdurakhmanov, a blogger and critic of the Chechen Republic who fled to Sweden. The attacker and an accomplice, both Russian citizens, were later convicted of attempted murder, where the attacker reiterated the fact that "he was acting on orders from Chechen officials". Others are keen to follow Sweden's lead. The Finnish Security and Intelligence Service (SUPO) has told me that refugee espionage has

Sweden has developed an expansive definition of transnational repression in its criminal code and called it refugee espionage or flyktingspionage

become a "permanent phenomenon in Finland", which represents a significant threat to national sovereignty: "If, for example, an illegal threat is done for the benefit of and on behalf of a foreign state, it violates not only the victim's rights, but also Finland's national sovereignty." This has led SUPO to lobby for it to be made a criminal offence in Finland. They have confirmed that it has been included in the new government's programme.

The UK is no stranger to threats against dissidents based in its territory either and in November 2022, the UK government announced the formation of the Defending Democracy Taskforce, chaired by Security Minister Tom Tugendhat, to review the UK's approach to transnational repression. Tugendhat has pledged to address the "activity of those who seek to stifle free expression in diaspora communities in the UK, those who try to silence the debate that they, as anyone else in the United Kingdom, should be able to enjoy." A Home Office spokesperson told me "attempts by foreign governments to coerce, intimidate, harass or harm their critics overseas, undermining democracy and the rule of law, are unacceptable. We are committed to tackling these challenges wherever they originate, which is why the Defending Democracy Taskforce is reviewing the UK's approach to transnational repression." But more than seven months later, little public progress has been made. For instance, threats to Iran International TV staff in London from the Iranian regime led the media outlet to flee to the USA, while Hong Kong issued arrest warrants and a bounty

for pro-democracy activists in exile, including some in the UK. These are just two glaring examples of transnational repression at work.

At the same time it is crucial to offer emotional and psychological support to the victims. Targets are expected to suffer in silence until a clearly defined crime has been committed. Beyond policing, Citizen Lab has recommended a number of tactics such as a "dedicated hotline and/or reporting mechanism for individuals to confidentially report instances of digital and other forms of transnational repression".

"Cyberspace does not lie within your borders." When John Perry Barlow wrote these words, the online world seemed to promise a freer space, a space too flexible to be controlled by existing modes of repression. But it is the authoritarian regimes, aided by private companies and calcified international laws, which have proved to be flexible enough to leverage online spaces. Cyberspace may not lie within their borders, but for them borders are not that important.

In the words of Lina al-Hathloul, the sister of imprisoned Saudi women's rights activist Loujain al-Hathloul, who was kidnapped and transported back to Saudi Arabia while driving in the UAE after years of online harassment and surveillance due to her activism for women's rights, "You are never really safe. You can always be targeted wherever you are." ✖

Nik Williams is policy and campaigns officer at Index

52(03):24/29|DOI:10.1177/03064220231201270

Peer pressure

In China, students are made to rate other students' political credentials. **THIỆN VIỆT** speaks to those who are refusing to do so

ABOVE: The 2023 graduation ceremony at China University of Petroleum in Qingdao, Shandong province

YUANYUAN, A SENIOR student at a prestigious university in Beijing, stands by her decision to refuse something that many of her classmates have conformed to: submitting an online self-evaluation and peer-evaluation report upon completing an academic year.

These evaluation forms are sent to all students at the beginning of a new academic year. While it is not indicated as being compulsory, students are obliged to complete them if they wish to be considered for campus-wide awards and honours or be nominated for opportunities such as research grants and conference trips.

Yuanyuan, which is a pseudonym, had underlying reasons not to do it.

It was not just the length, vagueness and repetition of the questions that deterred her but the fact that she would have to put a specific score on each and every one of her classmates – many of whom she had little interaction with.

"I feel terrible judging my classmates," she said. "I barely know them."

Interviews with 12 mainland Chinese students from seven universities testify to the common practice of peer evaluation. Every year, students enrolled at universities have to submit these forms, creating a toxic environment in which their peers feel they are being judged and reported on.

And it is only mainland Chinese students who are asked to do this. Yuanyuan's classmates from Hong Kong, Macao, Taiwan and other countries are exempt.

Anastasia, a Russian student enrolled on an English-taught programme at the same university as Yuanyuan, said that the international version of the evaluation form was much more simple.

"I do not have to compete with mainland students. International students are a separate category," she said.

Igor, from Brazil, shares the same

CREDIT: Cynthia Lee/Alamy

experience studying in Shanghai.

"We can nominate international peers for awards on certain occasions, but we never have to score them," he said.

Students have long been disgruntled by the forms. They ask students to evaluate their classmates in their designated *ban* (a class of around 30 or 50 students) on three vaguely- categorised aspects: academic attitude, mindset and morality and physical wellbeing.

"Other people's political attitude and wellbeing are none of my business," said Yuanyuan.

There is also a quota on the number of classmates that can be evaluated as "excellent" (usually up to 5% of the number of students in one class) which means they have to downgrade many classmates despite having no knowledge of their performances.

Hui, an MA student in Beijing, shares these concerns.

"How am I supposed to know whether my classmates are healthy or not, or whether they are ideologically 'normal?'" said Hui.

Sun, who is studying philosophy in Beijing, said that he did not take the peer evaluations seriously. He was not sure whether they were mandatory – and had not questioned them – but said that he did it to have peace of mind.

"You just have to give them scores," he said. "I do not think administrators would read them. They would use machines to calculate final scores for students."

He asked to be referred to by his last name only for privacy reasons, and said that he would try to give everyone the highest score possible so as to finish the evaluations quickly.

"Administrators would question you if you gave too many perfect scores," he said. "But I do not expect to receive a perfect score from anyone, either."

Students are pressured by their teachers to submit the reports. According to Yuanyuan, simply ignoring the forms is not enough.

Having not received her forms, an administrative officer sent her reminders

Administrators are not used to having students who say 'No' to them

via email and WeChat – China's most popular messaging system – to complete the two evaluations. Yet, having done it three times since her enrolment as an undergraduate student with little gain, Yuanyuan decided to say 'No'. In order to state her refusal, she had to go and meet the officer in person, explaining that considering her academic achievements and the competitiveness of the game, she didn't deem it worth her while.

Throughout the school year, students at her university have had to take different non-academic behavioural tests. During the pandemic, Yuanyuan was also asked by one of her teachers to do a patriotism test. She said that while her classmates were very uncomfortable doing the evaluations, very few dared to speak up.

"We are used to being oppressed," she said. "Administrators are not used to having students who say 'No' to them."

Hao Yue, a law graduate student from Shandong province, reluctantly carried out peer evaluation in order to achieve certain titles.

"I did not wish to miss out on opportunities, so I had to do that," he said. "Maybe we were taught to obey since we were [children]. We did not think about it."

Hui said she just marked everybody as "good".

"I just randomly chose some people I know to give them the highest scores, and the rest good," she said. "I just want to get it done."

Index approached administrators at seven universities in Beijing, most of whom refused to comment. But Guo, an administrator working for a Beijing-based university in charge of student affairs, did not conceal her frustration. Having had to do her own peer evaluation back in her university years, she said that she would run into trouble

with her superiors if she did not manage to collect students' evaluations on time.

"This is ridiculous, but what else can we do? It is a rule from above," said the 28-year-old, who added that she had to evaluate staff members, too.

Maria, who asked to be referred to by her English name, is no stranger to the task of evaluating her peers. In fact, she's required to self-evaluate and evaluate her fellow Communist Party members on a regular basis.

"We have to write about other party members as well," she said. "I will just write nice things for others, hoping that they might do the same for me."

However, for Hao, the law graduate, the loosely conducted peer evaluations reflect some hidden realities.

"If you are not on good terms with many people in your class, your scores will be noticeably lower," he said. "Administrators might pay attention to the less likable ones."

And Jiaxin, an economics student in Beijing, agreed: "You should not make inappropriate comments or have any conflict with your classmates. Otherwise, your classmates might lower your grades."

That said, Jiaxin believes that this peer evaluation is nothing more than a formality – an act of self-preservation where everyone will give good scores knowing they themselves are being evaluated.

Hao is less certain. Her academic environment is very competitive and she is not sure she can trust anyone beyond her close friends.

"It would be troublesome not to do it," she said. "Teachers and administrative officers would see you as disobedient." ✖

Thiện Việt is a journalist from Vietnam who writes under a pseudonym for safety reasons

52(03):30/31|DOI:10.1177/03064220231201271

No country for anxious men

Years of war have led to a mental health crisis in Yemen, but taboos abound. **LAURA SILVIA BATTAGLIA** visits the country's main mental health hospital to speak to its doctors and patients

ABDUSAMAD'S EYES MEET Yahya Faisal Hassan's gaze for 10 long seconds. In the suffocating humidity of the early afternoon, Abdusamad fears being restrained again in a cell. But today this is not going to happen: patient and doctor are making peace, in silence, in front of the iron door of the male section of the only psychiatric hospital in Yemen.

The walls of the dilapidated building, built in the 1970s in the capital of the south, Aden, are painted in two colours – white above a watery green. The colours promise relaxation but the difficulties of mental disorder show up in this place every day. The dream of every patient is to get out of here and never come back, but the reality, for Abdusamad and the other 150 patients, is the opposite: most of them have been forgotten by their families for months

or even years. Some have been here for as long as the war in Yemen has lasted. It began in 2015 and has not finished, despite some attempts at peace.

If you want to understand the long-term effects of the conflict in Yemen and the hard price the survivors have paid, there is no better health institution to visit. People say that if the war does not kill you, it will destroy your brain. Years of studies and research by several groups of experts back that up – studies such as those at the Dart Centre for Journalism and Trauma, which show how permanent the damage of the war can be on humans. PTSD is just one pathology on a long list.

Abdusamad is a perfect example: stimulated and then calmed by anti-psychotic drugs, he was in the "restraint" cell for a week. He had become aggressive, dangerous to himself and to other patients. As soon as he

came out, he looked for the doctor, Hassan, who put him in there.

"It is very difficult to be a psychiatrist in Yemen because we are trying to do our best with the few tools we have," Hassan told Index.

"But the patient is still a human being and we know that drugs and other old methods are not the best possible. We know what the restraint room means:

 Stimulated and then calmed by anti-psychotic drugs, he was in the "restraint" cell for a week

it is a prison. But what can we do? We have no other choices here."

He continues to sweat in his shirt and obsessively checks the tie, removed due to the merciless heat. In his anxiety, I read the sense of guilt of all the Yemeni medical class deprived of the essential tools for care: while the world and science move on, in Yemen mental health continues to be seen as madness. According to the World Health Organisation, 20% of the Yemeni population is affected by anxiety and depressive disorders, to mention only the most common. As Hassan shows me the "restraint room" – a bare, dirty cell, with a green mattress thrown into a corner – outside the building stand about 40 people, wanting to be admitted.

The manager of the hospital, Khalid al-Mahdi, is in trouble.

"We are the only psychiatric hospital across the country: every day we receive 400 requests of hospitalisation between Aden and the other Yemeni provinces where we also run small clinics. In these provinces the total population is 10 million people. Therefore, nobody will be surprised if we cannot provide a sufficient service. Not to mention that our budget was stopped at just over three million Yemeni rial per month (equal to $27,000), and the funds are totally insufficient," he said.

Al-Mahdi is a thin, well-dressed man in a suit. He knows the history of the hospital well. "From the 90s onwards there was a large decline of the structure," he said. "We were forgotten by the institutions. And this certainly had a negative impact on patients. We would need to restore it, to expand it, to host a higher number of patients; we would need greater quality of food, better medicines, modern methods of care."

The hospital was the first medical structure built in the south of the country – more open and progressive, but also more affected by poverty and marginalisation due to the politics of former president Ali Abdullah Saleh, who ruled Yemen for 33 years until

2011. Today the hospital is the physical proof that mental illness exists in Yemen, a country that denies its existence and has many who still believe that only spirits (*jinnis*) are responsible for any form of psychological or neurological distress, from depression to epilepsy.

Little wonder, then, that people suffering are still isolated in private homes or in "clinics". In some, patients are known to be in chains, such as in a facility in the city of Taiz. The war has simply worsened problems already present in the country. The social stigma is strong. Women pay the highest price: they're the least listened to by families, by doctors and in the hospital in Aden.

The hospital has beds for 125 men and only 25 women. Out of six departments, five are for males and only one is for females. Women typically stay in the hospital for a longer period: psychiatric disorders must be hidden, and a "crazy" woman is considered useless and unpresentable. Alisa, for example, is 41 and has been in and out of the hospital for 13 years. Kholood,

ABOVE AND OPPOSITE: Inside the main psychiatric hospital in Yemen

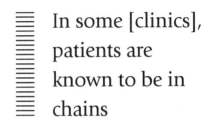

In some [clinics], patients are known to be in chains

a 40-year-old lawyer, is one of the few patients who agrees to speak. Her family lives in Aden but, for now, she prefers living here.

"I don't practise the profession because of my disorder. My family members come to visit me once every two months. But I like the fact that they take care of me and I'm happy to stay here," she said.

In addition to a lack of beds and money, thousands of others are unable to access care due to environmental and logistical factors. "Yemen is still a country in war, with blocks imposed by militias in the area," al-Mahdi said.

Then there are secondary impacts of the war, such as inflation and the destruction of the infrastructure.

So who can help treat this collective trauma? Certainly not the government or the militias, who are interested only in a population of young fighters and the women who give birth to them.

The queue of men and women in need of treatment at this hospital is destined to get longer. Many are former soldiers who have survived captivity and torture. They're traumatised and rejected by their families.

Behind a forced smile, 20-year-old Mohammad – destroyed by what he has witnessed – does not complain. "I collected with my own hands my comrade's brain, in pieces. He was a brother to me. How could I be anywhere else but here?" ✖

Laura Silvia Battaglia is a freelance award-winning journalist, living between Italy and Sanaa, Yemen

52(03):32/33|DOI:10.1177/03064220231201272

Nollywood gets naked

Nigeria's filmmakers are challenging the censorship board one breast at a time. The result is both provocative and engaging, writes **TILEWA KAZEEM**

AFRICA'S LOVE-HATE RELATIONSHIP with sex dates back centuries, long before the first African film, Borom Sarret (1963) by Senegalese director Sembène Ousmane, was ever made.

Rooted in a complex interplay of culture, religion and the lingering influences of colonisation, the continent's conservatism towards sexuality has historically sought to restrict and regulate everything that connotes sex or is overtly sexual. As institutions and laws were created to relegate discussions and portrayals of sex to the boudoir or the realm of taboo, an unintended consequence of silence emerged – one that would quietly govern how art, particularly the medium of film, was created, portrayed and consumed.

As a result, African filmmakers have long grappled with the challenges of censorship, compromising the authenticity of their narratives.

In Nigeria, one criterion a film or video submitted to the National Film and Video Censors Board (NFVCB) must pass with flying colours is that it "does not promote blasphemy or obscenity nor depict any matter which

is indecent, obscene or likely to be injurious to (public or private) morality or likely to incite or encourage public disorder or crime or is undesirable in the public interest".

The agency has demonstrated a proactive stance in promptly enforcing regulations pertaining to nudity in films, effectively ensuring compliance and upholding societal norms.

In a notable turn of events, the highly-anticipated release of the film adaptation of Chimamanda Ngozi Adichie's renowned novel Half of a Yellow Sun faced a delay in 2014. While initial reports suggested a complete ban by the NFVCB, industry insiders paint a different picture. FilmOne Distribution, a prominent distributor for the film, clarified that "the movie was not banned", emphasising that the delay stemmed from the need to obtain proper certification for public release. Set against the tumultuous backdrop of the Nigerian civil war in the 1960s and 1970s, this powerful adaptation explored themes of warfare, violence and sexuality. A scene filmed with Thandiwe Newton's breast exposed marked a significant step in Nigeria's cinematic expression of nudity.

Two years later, Netflix invested $148 million in film production in Africa. While this was mainly in South Africa, some of the money did go into Nigeria, signalling a transformative era and more good news for nudity in Nigeria.

Òlòtūré (2019), an intriguing film that delves into the harrowing world of human trafficking, marked Nigeria's tentative exploration of nudity with

> ≣ **A scene filmed with Thandiwe Newton's breast exposed marked a significant step**

a subtle and sparingly depicted scene showcasing various derrières. However, it was not until 2022, through the collaborative efforts of filmmaker Kunle Afolayan and Netflix, that nudity truly made its triumphant return to Nigerian cinema in the form of Aníkúlápó – a title meaning "one with death in his pouch" in the native Yoruba language.

In a controversial scene, lead characters Arolake (Bimbo Ademoye) and Saro (Kunle Remi) were depicted in a sexually intertwined manner, with Arolake's breasts and Saro's buttocks prominently displayed. This watershed moment sparked a powerful and transformative chain reaction, fuelling

ABOVE: A still from the film Òlòtūré, featuring Ikechukwu Onunaku (top) and Sharon Ooja (bottom)

the growth and inclusivity of nudity in the vibrant world of Nollywood.

The boundary-pushing nature of Afolayan's film has fostered a renaissance in Nollywood, inspiring filmmakers to delve into previously uncharted territory and shatter preconceived notions. The inclusion of nudity as a powerful storytelling tool has added a new dimension to African cinema, enhancing its authenticity and providing audiences with a more immersive and honest cinematic experience. Elesin Oba, The King's Horseman (2022), Shanty Town (2023), A Sunday Affair (2023) and Ijakumo: The Born Again Stripper (2022),

among an array of remarkable releases, stand as poignant testaments to the fruitful collaborations between African filmmakers and Netflix.

Amazon Prime Video, having entered the Nigerian market in 2020, has made remarkable strides in positioning itself as a prominent destination for top-tier Nigerian films. The streaming platform has not only offered a diverse selection of content but also delved into original productions, exemplified by the exclusive premiere of Gangs of Lagos earlier this year. This 18+ film, featuring a scene of borderline nudity, weaves the captivating narratives of a group of friends navigating their destinies amidst

the vibrant streets of Isale Eko.

While Gangs of Lagos marks its inaugural venture into original content, it is premature to anoint Amazon as a full liberator in the realm of nudity depiction. The responsibility for portraying nudity in a story still primarily resides with the directors, rather than being solely dictated by the streaming platform's choices. The evolving landscape of Nigerian cinema sees streaming services playing an influential role, but the artistic vision of the directors remains paramount in →

LEFT: Comfort Booth is skeptical about Nollywood's embrace of nudity

→ shaping the storytelling experience.

"The landscape has changed. The filmmaking process involves robust branches – the executive producer, the producer and the director – who keenly focus on the bottom line: return on investment. If the appetite calls for nudity, they will incorporate it, regardless of how the story is told," Comfort Booth told Index.

Booth – a lawyer, a cast member of The Real Housewives of Abuja and writer of Netflix film Love, Lust and Other Things – agrees that Nigeria's film industry is pushing boundaries.

"There is definitely a shift in the industry's approach to nudity – there's an increase and almost a desperation to incorporate the scenes. I am guessing for 'acceptability' on an international platform where anything goes," she said.

However, despite the writer's awareness of the growth of nudity in

Nudity is often used for exploitative purposes

Nollywood, in what she calls "almost a desperation to incorporate", she's conservative towards letting that influence her creativity. She said: "I will remain true to who I am and my principles. I don't believe in using nudity as a means to make the film real."

Her stance that "nudity is often used for exploitative purposes and to cater to viewers' guilty pleasures" is a qualm expressed not only by the writer. The nudity scenes shown in Aníkúlapó were greeted with considerable criticism – so much so that Remi took to Instagram to address the claims that the sex scenes in the film were "unnecessary". Remi said the scenes were the most "vulnerable moments for the characters" and a depiction of their love.

The eventual revelation that a prosthetic bosom was used instead of the actor's real breasts in the nude scenes opened a new artistic dimension to Nigerian cinema. Once deemed unfathomable, this technique, coupled with "nuancing" approaches, challenges censorship guidelines and fosters creativity. Beyond enhancing storytelling, it generates job opportunities for the production team and bolsters Nollywood's standing. Moreover, it ignites conversations among audiences, infusing the industry with a bold and dynamic spirit.

As Nigerian filmmakers continue to explore these avenues, they unravel the potential of unbridled creativity. This newfound artistic delight empowers the industry to embrace diverse narratives and thought-provoking discussions, cementing its place on the global stage. The future of Nigerian cinema shines brightly, powered by innovation and unapologetic storytelling. ✖

Tilewa Kazeem is a Nigerian sex columnist with an interest in culture stories

52(03):34/36|DOI:10.1177/03064220231201283

Policing symbolism

Protest art has come under fire since Peru's political crisis
hit breaking point, writes **JIMENA LEDGARD**

EVERY HOLY WEEK, the streets of the main square in Ayacucho, a small Peruvian city in the central Andes, are covered with carpets crafted from flowers and dyed sawdust to celebrate the most sacred dates in the Catholic calendar.

This year, there was one that stood out among the traditional religious scenes and motifs: a minimalistic design featuring a large black cross with the words "*No Mataras*" – "Thou shalt not kill" – and "December 15, 2022".

The carpet referenced the killing of 10 civilians by the army in Ayacucho, a day after president Dina Boluarte authorised the armed forces to intervene in ongoing protests against her government, even though military personnel are not trained to deal with civilians in the context of social unrest. Their response included using helicopters to drop tear gas and firing live ammunition at unarmed protesters. The youngest victim was 15 years old.

"We had the carpet made to remind everyone that Holy Week was not holy, that it was tainted by all the blood that had been spilled and the lack of justice," Ruth Barcena told Index.

Barcena is the president of a collective formed by relatives of those killed and wounded on 15 December and organised around a demand for justice and accountability.

Barcena's husband, 32-year-old driver Leonardo Hancco, was among those fatally injured by the army. He'd joined the protests, carrying a sign demanding a new constitution for his country. Barcena recalls rushing downtown after hearing he'd been injured.

"It was like being in hell," she said. "They were running after people and shooting them in the street."

Hancco died that day and, shortly after, the pregnant Barcena lost the twin babies she was carrying.

Commissioning a carpet to commemorate the deaths was a way of dealing with the paralysing grief she still struggles with. After unveiling it, however, the group was immediately surrounded by police.

"They trampled all over it. We were too scared to fight back. We were afraid we'd be killed as well," Barcena recalled. "All we could do was stand to one side and cry."

The police detained those involved in the making of the carpet and threatened them with prosecution, although all charges were eventually dropped. Nevertheless, the incident highlights a worrying trend by the government of censoring forms of symbolic and creative protest, stigmatising those in opposition and curtailing freedom of expression, according to the protesters and human rights activists who spoke to Index.

The ongoing political crisis has had grave consequences for basic civil rights in the country. Between 2022 and 2023,

> ABOVE: Political cartoonist César Aguilar's *La Descarada* float joins a parade, and has now been destroyed

Peru fell 33 positions on the latest World Press Freedom Index and is currently ranked 110th out of 180 countries. In the last two weeks of July, at least nine journalists suffered police violence or were subject to arbitrary detentions while covering the latest wave of anti-government protests, according to Reporters Without Borders.

Filmmaker and photographer Kenty Aguirre was detained and held in police custody for 43 hours and was left with bruises and abrasions on his body. Just a few days earlier, a university student was arbitrarily accused of writing "*Dina Asesina*" ("Dina the murderer") on a wall and, whilst detained, suffered a serious asthma attack, requiring hospital treatment.

In June, political cartoonist César Aguilar, along with students and fellow professors from the National University Diego Quispe Tito in Cusco, created a float for the city's annual university parade.

Named *La Descarada* – a play on words that means both "the shameless woman" and "the faceless woman" – it referenced Boluarte by depicting a woman dressed in military garb, stepping over skulls.

The float became a viral sensation throughout the country, which might have contributed to Aguilar reportedly facing ongoing threats by the →

Their response included using helicopters to drop tear gas and firing live ammunition at unarmed protesters

→ authorities. When *La Descarada* disappeared the day after the parade, he said he learned from other professors that it had been taken by university personnel and burned.

"The minister of education then pressured the university to force me to sign a public letter apologising to the president and the government," he told Index. "After I refused to sign, the university started a new recruitment process for my position halfway through the academic year, which is entirely irregular."

Aguilar also denounced censorship against El Muro ("The Wall") – a grassroots organisation he co-founded that highlights topics of civic interest by posting printed news, political commentary and art on a wall in downtown Cusco.

Despite working without interruption for the past two decades, he claims that police now prevent them from conducting their usual activities, effectively limiting freedom of expression in a country where many still don't have access to social media or other forms of online discussions.

Activists and protesters from Lima, the country's capital, have not been spared this form of censorship and prosecution, either. In January, shortly after the police fatally shot 18 people in the city of Juliaca, young actress Leonor Estrada staged a theatrical protest in solidarity with those killed.

Donning a wig and a presidential sash draped over an oversized suit, she trampled and danced over a Peruvian flag during a small demonstration in the upscale district of Miraflores. Assuming the persona of Boluarte, Estrada shouted

Estrada shouted at police: "Do you want to shoot? Go ahead!"

RIGHT: 11 January 2023 in Juliaca, Peru, people commemorate protesters who were killed after heavy clashes with police two days before in the same city. The protests were directed against the government of interim President Boluarte, with the demonstrators demanding her resignation

at police: "Do you want to shoot? Go ahead! Shoot them! Aim straight for their bodies!"

Shortly after, a group of lawyers brought her case to the attention of the judiciary on charges of insulting patriotic symbols. The offence is categorised as a criminal charge and carries a sentence of up to four years.

Estrada's lawyer, Gabriela Paliza, told Index that the investigation was still ongoing. "We argue that this does not constitute an attack only on freedom of expression but on the right to exercise your craft," she said. "Leonor is a performance actress, but this is extremely difficult to explain in Peruvian courts."

Jennie Dador, the executive secretary of the National Coordinator of Human Rights coalition, underscores that these actions collectively constitute a clear effort to curtail freedom of expression and dissenting voices in the country. Dador said prosecutors were well aware that these charges were likely to be ultimately dismissed or archived.

"Still, the person is subjected to unreasonable and draining investigations that can stretch for multiple years," she told Index. "Ultimately, this exerts a self-censoring impact on society as a whole, acting as a sort of disciplinary mechanism to regulate what can and cannot be said."

Aguilar agrees. "We are internalising the notion that it's best not to disturb power – to just mind your own business."

State efforts to stigmatise symbolic dissent, however, can sometimes backfire, leading to widespread mockery.In March, police in Lima seized makeshift shields employed by protesters to protect themselves against tear gas and rubber bullets during protests. The shields are often made by members of the Primera Línea, a loosely-organised collective

of protesters inspired by the tactics displayed in Hong Kong. Seen as either anonymous heroes or dangerous agents of terror, they often rush to deactivate tear gas and don't shy away from physically clashing with law enforcement.

At a press conference, police commander Jorge Angulo proudly showed one of the seized shields,

adorned with red, black and yellow letters that spelled "BOYKA" – purportedly referring to the name of an American-Bulgarian martial arts film franchise. Gesturing towards the shield, he said: "Semiotics enables us to decode messages through symbols and colours. In this case, the red letter signifies violence, the black letter signifies death and the yellow letter signifies happiness. This is by no means coincidental."

The statements made by the facetiously-labelled "semiotics police officer" led to widespread mockery on social media. However, a member of Primera Línea – speaking to Index on condition of anonymity – said they felt more concern than amusement.

"It almost feels like they hyperfocus on things that are not really a threat to them. Graffiti, words, symbols, shields... they're trying to repress even harmless dissent." ✖

Jimena Ledgard is a journalist and producer based in Lima, Peru

52(03):37/39|DOI:10.1177/03064220231201284

Setting the story straight

DANSON KAHYANA has witnessed how Ugandan laws against promoting homosexuality are stifling creativity. Here he sits down with a student of his to ask them about censoring their own work

ONE OF THE most unfortunate aspects of Uganda's 2023 Anti-Homosexuality Act (AHA) is that it criminalises creativity and scholarship. If a writer or filmmaker publishes a work with homoerotic content, it could be construed as promoting homosexuality, they could be prosecuted and, if found guilty, they could be imprisoned "for a period not exceeding 20 years".

Had the acclaimed Ugandan writer Jennifer Nansubuga Makumbi published her novel Kintu in Uganda after May 2023, she might have been prosecuted for promoting homosexuality. In that classic, she creates a bisexual character called Ssentalo, a general in the Kabaka's (or Buganda king's) army, who makes his preference for male lovers clear when he says that sleeping with a fellow man "is like a river: a one-way flow for many people, no return. Once you have heard the hoarse groan of a man, felt the moist hairy skin and drunk the scent of male sweat you will not want to hold a woman again".

Under the AHA, the fact that Makumbi's novel has a character with such pro-homosexuality views could be construed to mean that she is promoting homosexuality, thereby making her liable to prosecution and imprisonment. Luckily for her, the novel was published in 2014 (the year Uganda's constitutional court declared a similar law discriminatory and illegal), and in neighbouring Kenya (where such a law does not exist at the moment). She lives in the democratic UK, not

> The work's LGBTQ+ content and themes could lead the library and library staff into trouble under the provisions of the AHA

in repressive Uganda. But what about booksellers such as Aristoc Booklex in Kampala which stock this book? And libraries such as Makerere University Library which have copies of this book? What about scholars such as Dr Edgar Fred Nabutanyi and me who have taught this book to students at our home base, Makerere University, and given conference talks and written scholarly articles on it, some of them highlighting the author's depictions of homosexuality? Are we safe from prosecution and imprisonment for promoting homosexuality?

It might seem that I am asking rhetorical questions in the fashion of a literary analyst, but I am not. Under Article 11 of the AHA, anyone who knowingly advertises, publishes, prints, broadcasts or distributes "any material promoting or encouraging homosexuality" is committing an offence. Under this act, creativity and scholarship have been criminalised.

On 16 June 2023, a creative-writing student who I taught for two semesters presented his corrected undergraduate project to me entitled A Rainbow Manifesto and The Bells of a Creative Mind. The project broached LGBTQ+ themes in a bold way. In one of the poems, he castigated society's boxing of people into neat gender roles, for instance the expectation that "a boy must not like pink and all those cute 'girl' things" such as wearing high-heeled shoes.

In others, he boldly addressed the people who asked if he were gay or straight: "If my appearance brings you discomfort / stay away from the people and things that bring me comfort / The way I express my love is unique, don't make it your goal to understand it."

Sometimes he got angry when addressing homophobic people: "Whoever told these idiots / that what they practise is normal / must have been a cunty one."

He made it clear that he did not tolerate homophobia: "For now, you can

 # I fear that I could be arrested and prosecuted, in case the librarian has reported me to the police

bend over and we show you where to put all your noise / For the more you fight us, the more we change from what you knew yesterday / You can hate as much as you want / but the love we have for who we are is bigger than you can imagine."

When he presented the project to the library for digital archiving (which is a submission requirement), a librarian assigned it a digital object identifier. The student was happy – his fears that the library could censor his work in the wake of the AHA had proven unfounded. Unfortunately, his happiness was short-lived. A week later, his work was pulled down from the university library's website. When he asked why, the librarian told him the reason: the work's LGBTQ+ content could lead the library and library staff into trouble under the provisions of the AHA. The librarian's advice? "If you want your work uploaded, edit it and remove all traces of homosexual content."

Afraid of being prosecuted for promoting homosexuality and eager to get his bachelor's degree, the student did as the librarian had asked him to. He changed the titles of his poems and purged the work of LGBTQ+ content and themes. He told me: "I revised the language and removed the words or phrases that were in line with the topic that had been rejected by the library. The new version of my work is 'straight' and doesn't communicate anything in line with what was being addressed in my previous work. For example, the poem Alienated, Affected in my original work talks about how same-sex relationships are despised, condemned and stigmatised by straight people, while the new version, Lost Affection, simply talks about hate in general and what it's taking away from the world. The focus

is not homophobia, but love for one another and the world at large in order to make it a better place."

The library's action of deleting the student's work has affected him in a number of ways. He said: "My confidence and self-esteem were lowered and I don't feel safe away from my home – I fear that I could be arrested and prosecuted, in case the librarian has reported me to the police. I have realised that I cannot write what I want; I have to be careful about what I think and what I put on paper. Basically, my freedom is under attack. My mental health is at stake; I sleep less. On some nights, I find myself waking up and deeply thinking about this whole situation."

What is clear is that under the provisions of the AHA – particularly Article 11 – it is now illegal to imagine a world in which characters practise homosexuality. As a writer, filmmaker or visual artist, your work must be straight through and through, lest you risk spending up to 20 years in prison for committing the offence of promoting homosexuality.

In other words, the Ugandan state, through its parliament, has legislated what US poet Adrienne Rich called "compulsory heterosexuality". It has declared homosexuality deviant and abhorrent, and threatened to punish any creative writer who dares imagine a world where lesbianism, bisexuality, homosexuality, pan-sexuality or anything other than heterosexuality is possible. By doing this, it has criminalised certain forms of creativity. ✖

Danson Kahyana is East Africa's contributing editor for Index. He is based in Uganda.

52(03):40/41|DOI:10.1177/03064220231201286

A marriage made in transgression

ALEXANDRA DOMENECH speaks to one of the few outspoken dissidents who has not fled Russia

ALEXANDRA POPOVA CANNOT be alone anymore. The democracy activist, who is also a painter, spoke to Index from Moscow nine months after security forces tortured her and poet Artyom Kamardin, who was then her fiancé, in their home. "To this day, I constantly feel the need to be around my friends," she said.

It was last September when police officers raided the couple's apartment, sexually assaulted Kamardin, beat him up and forced him to apologise on camera. Meanwhile, Popova was held captive in the next room. The officers repeatedly punched her, put glue on her face and threatened her with rape.

They also showed her photographs they had taken of Kamardin's injuries. "That was part of their plan, which was to humiliate us," she said.

Kamardin was thrown into detention immediately afterwards, but Popova was released without charge.

The day before they were targeted, Kamardin recited a satirical poem about Russia invading Ukraine at the Mayakovsky Readings, a gathering of dissident poets in central Moscow which took place regularly during the Soviet era. Popova believes the authorities felt they needed to punish him for doing so.

"After what [the police] had done to him, they were expecting him to remain silent and plead guilty," she said.

The poet is now on trial, charged with inciting hatred and actions against state security, and facing up to 10 years in prison. During his court appearances, Kamardin highlighted how the torment was affecting his physical and mental health, describing symptoms including persistent back pain, stomach aches and panic attacks.

But the couple did not give in. Popova filed a complaint with the

LEFT: Alexandra Popova is arrested for wearing a mask reading "freedom" during protests supporting journalist Ilya Azar in 2020. Behind her is Dmitry Ivanov, since sentenced to eight years for speaking out

LEFT: Alexandra Popova with police in 2020; ABOVE: Popova and her now husband, who is currently in jail

CREDIT: Provided by Alexandra Popova; (Popova and Kamardin) Andrey Trager

Investigative Committee against those who were involved in torturing them, but it refused to open a criminal case despite the evidence.

"The authorities would never betray their own people, especially those who are capable of murder," she said, adding that she felt their tormentors "are capable of killing somebody".

Popova has relentlessly drawn the public's attention to the human rights violations that Kamardin suffered upon arrest and while in prison.

Despite "a brain concussion and multiple wounds", she said he was deprived of medical treatment and Popova suspects the police exerted pressure on the doctors to refuse his admission to hospital.

Later, the poet was sent to a psychiatric facility for a month, held with a man charged with murder.

"It's a common practice. Its purpose is to make the whole experience even more nerve-racking," Popova said.

We were fighting for a democratic society, where human life would matter

Since his arrest Kamardin has also not received proper psychiatric help. The prison doctor prescribed him only with what Popova described as a Soviet-era antidepressant with many serious side effects.

To make matters worse, books have not been allowed into the prison since February "because the [prison] governor decided so". Popova said, "Artyom suffers a lot from the lack of literature."

But she did win two battles against prison authorities by putting pressure on them. Today Kamardin can get time in the open air on a regular basis, which he was not allowed to do for many months. The couple also married in May, even though the prison authorities "repeatedly" lost their documents.

It was not the first time that Popova had dealt with a prison administration. She has been supporting political prisoners for five years, organising letter-writing events, co-ordinating the sending of parcels and observing court hearings.

She said the situation of political prisoners in Russia was depressing, explaining that "prolonged incarceration is killing many of them. Torture is becoming increasingly normalised. I have heard of multiple cases of electric-shock torture of political prisoners, especially anarchists."

Did she ever feel that there would be a brighter future? She recalled that in 2018, when she took part in

demonstrations supporting opposition leader Alexey Navalny, she felt "something was starting to shift".

"We were fighting for a democratic society, where human life would matter and we would not be imprisoned for speaking up; where we would live in peace, without the police barging into our homes in the morning," she said.

But in the following years the number of people imprisoned for joining protests grew rapidly, and "the free space shrank further and further".

For Popova, there is not much hope left. She said: "In the future things could get even scarier."

She added that she wished political prisoners could avoid serving their full sentences and be released early.

Despite constant surveillance by the authorities, Popova will stay in Moscow. "Artyom needs me. Other political prisoners need me, too. Who will take care of them if everyone leaves?"

And asked if she feared the consequences of speaking up, she responded: "I have already seen the worst that can happen.

"The only thing that terrifies me today is remaining silent." ✖

Alexandra Domenech is a Moscow-born, Paris-based journalist specialising in women's rights in Russia

52(03):42/43|DOI:10.1177/03064220231201289

Out of the oven, into the fire

Rohingya Muslims thought they were reaching safety in India, but under Narendra Modi their future is precarious. **MIR AIYAZ** reports from a Delhi refugee camp

CREDIT: Pankaj Nangia/Anadolu Agency

T IS 4.30 in the afternoon and Sulaiman, who has just turned four, is sitting cross-legged beside his maternal aunt Sabira in a tarpaulin-roofed shack in a slum in Madanpur Khadar, south Delhi.

Three years ago, like many other Rohingya refugees in India, his parents were taken by the police from their camp.

"My sister had offered prayers and prepared tea at around seven in the morning. Along with her husband, they were about to begin their breakfast when a community leader knocked on the door asking them to come along because police had asked for both of them to show up at a metro station," recalled Sabira, the elder of the two sisters.

Once at the station, according to Sabira, the couple were bundled into a car, never to return. They were taken to a detention centre, despite possessing a refugee card provided by the UN High Commission for Refugees, and for years were not allowed to meet their child. Only now are they allowed to see him, but he is still somewhat inexplicably not allowed to live with them.

Of course what most pains Sabira and others in the family is the impact it has had on Sulaiman, a child being kept away from the love and affection of his parents at such a young age.

"Sulaiman often weeps and asks 'When will my mother come?'" said Sabira of a boy who has little confidence and who barely speaks in front of strangers.

Saying goodbye to the lush green fields of Rakhine, a state in Myanmar, to move to a fetid slum such as the one they are in today in Delhi was hard, but essential for Sulaiman's family. The Muslim Rohingya have faced extreme and regular discrimination due to their distinct ethnicity, religion and language compared with the majority Buddhist Burmans.

During 2016 and 2017, a genocide unfolded, resulting in the deaths of

LEFT: Over 50 shanties were gutted after a fire broke out at a Rohingya refugee camp in New Delhi, India on June 13, 2021

around 9,000 Rohingyas, who had endured discrimination for decades. The Rohingya community was subjected to appalling atrocities, including forced labour, torture and disappearances. The US State Department's report in 2018 shed light on these heinous acts and the violence extended to the brutal rape, abuse and murder of Rohingya women, leading the UN to label them as the world's "most persecuted minority".

Calm before another storm

For many Rohingya Muslims, who reached India before the right-wing government of the Bharatiya Janata Party led by Prime Minister Narendra Modi came to power, things went smoothly without any fear of deportation. They got work and, more importantly, refuge from persecution.

"When I reached Delhi, I took a deep breath, feeling a sigh a relief. I was sure now things will be good because I had heard about Nizamuddin Dargah [a mausoleum for a Muslim saint in Delhi] in my younger days," said Fareed, who is now in his mid-30s.

Fareed got a job, saved some money and then got married. "The initial phase in India was good. There was no threat of deportation and we were going about our business as usual," he said.

But once vigilante justice was stirred up on social media under Modi, with Muslims being lynched in broad daylight, the call for deportation of Muslims who came from Myanmar grew louder. Fear set in. Many started wondering whether they had made the right choice.

Fareed recalled one incident: "One day after BJP came to power in 2014, a Hindu man who used to work with me as a labourer said: 'We will keep you suppressed'."

The people who spoke to Index did not want to use their full names in case of repercussions, but they all told similar stories.

"Many people of our community were killed, along with my father in Myanmar. He was in his shop at around 11pm when he was killed by the police," said Ismaiel, who came to India via Bangladesh back in 2012. Still, life in India today is tough.

"The opportunities are not here," said Ismaiel. "We are not able to teach our children the way we would have wanted."

The camp that he and Fareed, Sulaiman and Sabira are in has been set on fire several times. Conditions are squalid, food scarce and security lax.

All the while, India refuses to recognise Rohingyas as refugees and intentionally stirs up xenophobia. Last September, the central government denied documentation for a Rohingya woman and her children, who sought to join their father in the USA. During a court proceeding in Delhi, the government asserted that Rohingya refugees living in India posed a serious threat to the country's national security.

Back in 2018, the government said that the Rohingya community had links to terrorist organisations when justifying their stance on "illegal immigrants" in front of the Supreme Court. Television channels and media aligned with the government amplified these allegations without evidence, further contributing to the unjust criminalisation of the Rohingya community.

This has had severe consequences, as India threatens to deport Rohingya refugees for lacking valid travel documents, violating the international legal principle of non-refoulement, which prevents the forced return of refugees to countries where they may face harm or persecution.

Though India is not a party to the UN Convention Relating to the Status of Refugees (1951) and its 1967 Protocol, the principle of non-refoulement is universally recognised as binding on all countries. And India is a signatory to the Universal Declaration of Human Rights 1948, the International Covenant on Civil and Political Rights 1966, the 1989 UN Convention on the Rights of the Child and other international instruments that explicitly establish rights for detainees, especially women and children.

Although India's refugee protection obligations remain limited, the global consensus on non-refoulement remains a fundamental tenet of international law, obliging all countries to safeguard the rights and safety of asylum seekers, including the Rohingya.

For the last three years, Sabira has knocked on every possible door to secure the release of her sister. She has spoken to the police and officials, but no one will help. The innocent face and repeated questions of her nephew pierce her heart, adding to the grief that besieges the whole community.

Sitting next to Sabira is her elder daughter, Noor Fatima, who was born in India, far away from her ancestral home-state. When asked whether she would prefer to go back to Myanmar where her grandparents are, the primary school pupil says, "Yes, I would like to meet them in person."

Watching her daughter speak from a distance, Sabira interrupts: "However, this is not possible."

India's Rohingyas are trapped; unable to return to Myanmar, increasingly threatened in their new home and with no one willing to listen or help. ✖

Many started wondering whether they had made the right choice

Mir Aiyaz is a journalist based in India

52(03):44/45|DOI:10.1177/03064220231201293

23–26 NOVEMBER 2023

FOLLOW YOUR CURIOSITY

A PLACE WHERE IDEAS FLOW FREELY.
WHERE INSPIRATION FINDS YOU AT EVERY TURN.
A WINTER WONDERLAND OF IDEAS.
FOR ONE. FOR MANY. FOR ALL.
DISCOVER MORE AT
HAYFESTIVAL.ORG/WINTER-WEEKEND

@HAYFESTIVAL > #HAYWINTERWEEKEND

HAY
FESTIVAL
WINTER WEEKEND

SPECIAL REPORT

"The other man, eager to teach the new boy from the village a lesson, reported him to Hisbah, the Islamic police"

KOLA ALAPINNI | SHARIA LAW AND DISORDER | P.73

CREDIT: Kola Sulaimon / AFP

For the love of God?

REBECCA L ROOT explores the world's increasingly harsh blasphemy laws and speaks to those who have fallen foul of them

"IF CRYING COULD bring Mubarak back, I think maybe my cries would have brought him back [by now]."

On 28 April 2020, six weeks after Amina Ahmed had given birth to her son, her husband Mubarak Bala was taken away. It would be nine months before a letter, smuggled out of prison, would let her know that he'd been arrested and accused of blasphemy.

"My life has not been the same. I've gone through severe mental and psychological trauma," she told Index from her home in Nigeria. "This is wickedness of the highest order."

Two years after being arrested, Bala – an atheist from the predominantly Muslim state of Kano – was sentenced to 24 years in prison.

Around the globe, laws about blasphemy continue to be strictly enforced and strengthened with supporting legislation. The United States Commission on International Religious Freedom (USCIRF) said in a press release in May that it was "alarmed by the continued enforcement of blasphemy provisions".

"Blasphemy laws are [increasingly] implemented with higher punishments," Alexis Deswaef, vice president of the International Federation for Human Rights (FIDH), told Index.

Between 2014 and 2018, there were 732 reported blasphemy-related incidents in 41 countries. This is in spite of repeated calls from the UN to repeal blasphemy laws in order to make way for freedom of religion or belief. But that in itself is in conflict with the

UN Human Rights Council, who just adopted a resolution that "underscores the need" to hold individuals responsible for blasphemy to account, a move following protests that erupted after the burning of the Koran in Sweden. In July, a cohort of NGOs expressed concern that things could worsen if the UN approved the resolution. In a public letter calling for the draft to be rejected, the non-profits said the resolution "seeks to protect not only individuals but rather religious books and symbols" and that this is "contrary to guarantees of freedom of opinion and expression".

Since 2015, only nine countries have repealed blasphemy laws. And, as of 2020, 84 countries still had them – with penalties ranging from fines and imprisonment to capital punishment. Some countries have even strengthened their laws over the last year, while Denmark announced this summer plans to reintroduce theirs.

Iran and Pakistan, Muslim-majority countries, have the strictest blasphemy laws, as does Nigeria, which is divided between Muslim and Christian regions.

"Every religion should be strong enough to accept some critics, but what you see in a lot of countries that implement laws is that there are no critics of the main religion," Deswaef said, adding that blasphemy laws go hand-in-hand with apostasy laws, which prohibit individuals from renouncing their religion. →

LEFT: A veiled woman asks another woman without a mandatory headscarf to observe her hijab, at the Imam Khomeini mosque in downtown Tehran during the International Book Fair in May 2023

 Today it's Iran, tomorrow it could be somewhere else

→ This is exactly what Bala did. In 2014, Bala told his family he was no longer a believer in Islam. In response, they had him detained in a psychiatric facility. He was released shortly after and became president of the Nigerian Humanist Association, posting online about there being no afterlife.

He pleaded guilty to 18 counts of causing a public disturbance through "blasphemous" Facebook posts in accordance with the Kano State Penal Code. He could have received the death penalty if tried under Sharia law, in place in 12 of the country's northern states.

Iranian blogger and photojournalist Soheil Arabi did receive a ruling under Sharia law in Iran when he was sentenced to death in 2014 for posting articles on Facebook that criticised the Islamic government.

"In mid-autumn of 2013, 10 Islamic Revolutionary Guard Corps executioners stormed my photography studio [and] arrested me with guns and violence," he told Index, adding that he was then beaten and blindfolded.

If we protest, we will be recognised as infidels

"After 200 days of interrogation and explanation of accusations of blasphemy, proselytising activity against the system and insulting the Prophet of Islam, I was sentenced to the death penalty in the Islamic court."

His sentence was later changed to eight years in prison, and although he was released in 2021, Arabi has been forced to live in internal exile in a remote location.

In May 2023, two men who weren't successful in getting their sentences changed – Yusef Mehrdad and Seyyed Sadrullah Fazeli Zare – were executed in Iran for posts in a group chat on the Telegram app which were seen as insulting towards the Prophet Muhammad. In June, a 19-year-old man identifying as Christian was sentenced to

death in Pakistan for a similar incident.

And back in Nigeria, Islamic gospel singer Yahaya Sharif-Aminu was sentenced to death in 2020 by a Sharia court for blaspheming in a song. His case is set to be retried following complaints about the handling of the original trial.

Although Bala didn't receive the death penalty, Ahmed said she knew instinctively there'd be repercussions for him when she saw his online content. "I told him: 'I have a bad feeling that they are coming to get you'," she said.

But he refused to believe he could be arrested for posting on Facebook.

Imprisonment for blasphemy is becoming more common around the world. In June, Pong – who uses a pseudonym – was sentenced to 18

BELOW: The youngest son of factory manager Priyantha Kumara Diyawadana stands in front of the coffin of his father in Ganemulla, Sri Lanka in December 2021. Diyawadana was earlier beaten to death and set ablaze by a mob in Pakistan who accused him of blasphemy

CREDIT: Pacific Press Media Production Corp/Alamy

years in jail in Thailand, accused of posting insulting content about the monarchy, which is protected under law "in a position of revered worship". In March, a 19-year-old was sentenced to compulsory labour in Russia for burning a religious icon. And in 2021, a Yemeni man received a 15-year prison sentence in Saudi Arabia for renouncing his beliefs on Twitter. Foreigners there have also been accused of blasphemy, receiving up to 500 lashes and prison time as punishment.

Despite global outrage and calls from human rights organisations advocating for the release of these people, some countries have instead reinforced their existing blasphemy laws.

This year both houses of parliament in Pakistan passed legislation making it illegal to insult not only Islam and the Prophet Muhammad but also those connected to the Prophet. In Indonesia, a new criminal code passed in December 2022 has seen the blasphemy law extended to include apostasy for the first time. And in Iran, it was reported earlier this year that the Islamic criminal code was being adapted to criminalise sharing critical opinions on social media.

Misuse of blasphemy laws

Mahmood Amiry-Moghaddam, director of the NGO Iran Human Rights, believes the current Iranian regime is trying "to rebuild a barrier of fear" and is using the death penalty and blasphemy laws to do so. And as Deswaef has highlighted, blasphemy laws and their corresponding punishments are also being used to persecute minority groups.

Civilians pushed back on the authoritarian government with widespread protests last year when a young Kurdish woman, Jina "Mahsa" Amini, was killed in police custody having been arrested for not wearing the hijab in a way considered suitable.

"Blasphemy means that the government has the right to do any injustice to us, and if we protest we will be recognised as infidels and [it]

has the right to execute us," Arabi said, adding that there were also other repercussions.

"These regressive laws affect our whole lives, our studies, our work, our social relationships and even our romantic relationships. My wife divorced me, and I haven't seen my daughter for six years."

Isa Sanusi, Amnesty International's acting Nigeria director, explained how it was not unusual for people to take the law into their own hands. He described how a man with a mental health condition had been murdered.

"Someone dragged him into an argument. He said something and he was accused of blasphemy. People gathered around, set him on fire and killed him," he said, adding that such incidents were on the rise.

In June, Usman Buda, a butcher, was stoned to death in north-west Nigeria after getting into an altercation with another trader and being accused of blasphemy. And in February, a mob in eastern Pakistan lynched a man who was accused of the same crime.

According to USCIRF, of the 732 blasphemy-related incidents reported between 2014 and 2018 mob activity, violence or threats occurred in 78 cases that coincided with state enforcement and in 58 cases where there was no official enforcement.

Bala, too, was subjected to these activities, receiving threats to "chop off his head". Yet once he was sentenced, some who had been critical of his actions reached out to share that they thought the sentence was too harsh.

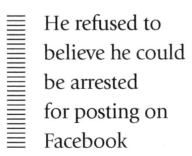

He refused to believe he could be arrested for posting on Facebook

"People take pity on him," Ahmed said, adding that Bala was doing as well as he could in prison, and calling for others outside Nigeria to urge the government to release her husband.

Setting an example

In April, the European Parliament said blasphemy laws in Nigeria were in violation of its international human rights commitments, the African Charter and the Nigerian constitution, and urged the authorities to release Bala as well as Sharif-Aminu and others. It also called on the country to lead the way in abolishing blasphemy laws.

But Amiry-Moghaddam said such an outcry never came when the two men in Iran were hanged. "We were expecting strong international reactions and those reactions didn't come," he said, adding that it sent an "unfortunate signal to all those who are threatening freedom of expression everywhere else".

"Today it's Iran, tomorrow it could be somewhere else," he said. He suggested that other countries impose sanctions on the judges involved in the case. "We need both strong diplomatic reactions and practical steps."

Arabi echoed this sentiment and stressed that political prisoners need international support. He said: "The Iranian government must be pressured to release the people."

Researchers have also called on social media companies to protect their users and "uphold global standards of free speech".

In the meantime, in Nigeria, Ahmed holds onto the hope that her husband will be released and get to witness at least some of his son's childhood.

"Let him be free and let him reconcile with his family. That is what I'm begging the Nigerian government for," she said. "It's insane. It's not right." ✖

Rebecca L Root is a freelance journalist based in Bangkok

52(03):48/51|DOI:10.1177/03064220231201295

CREDIT: Michael Nigro/Pacific Press/ZUMA Press Wire/Alamy

Worshippers of power

In the first of two interviews with experts on the rise of the religious right in the USA, **JEMIMAH STEINFELD** talks to **MARGARET ATWOOD** about the increasing use of religion as a weapon by the power-hungry

T IS HARD to argue with God, explains Margaret Atwood when asked about why the right often use religion to justify their actions.

"If you can accuse your enemies of heresy and blasphemy it's somehow more potent than accusing them of not agreeing with you politically," said the bestselling writer in an interview with Index.

"You're not just disagreeing with Mr Sunak, you're disagreeing with God," she said – and that's a big deal.

It has been more than six years since Atwood and I last spoke. In our last conversation, in 2017, Donald Trump was new to the White House. He's there no longer and, in fact, he's in a jail in Georgia as I type. But the people who

helped usher Trump into power – the white evangelicals – are, if anything, stronger. Roe v Wade, the 1973 Supreme Court ruling that found the right to an abortion is a constitutional one, has been repealed. The number of books

Instead of just saying "You're going to fry in hell", they mobilised

LEFT: Two Christian protesters pray together across the street from a restaurant holding a drag brunch, April 2023 in Chardon, Ohio

Any weapon that you devise will be used against you

being banned in libraries and schools across the USA because they "offend" this group is growing. Atwood is unwavering. "Without a doubt" she says when asked if people are using religion in a more emboldened way today than they were a decade ago.

Growing up in Canada – a nation that does not separate church and state in the way the USA historically has – Atwood is very familiar with religion. She read the Bible daily at school. Then, studying English literature at university demanded a familiarity with the Old and the New Testaments.

"In order to study those things and everything in between, you had to know quite a lot about the history and dogmas of Christianity because otherwise you couldn't understand it," she said.

Atwood's works are imbued with religious references, The Handmaid's Tale being the classic example. But contrary to what those who want the book banned say, it is not anti-religion. Far from it. Ofred, the main handmaid, recounts a self-styled Lord's Prayer in private and Methodists provide help to those escaping Gilead. Indeed, the book's entire premise is partly inspired by the section of the Bible, in Matthew, where it says "Beware of false prophets, who come to you in sheep's clothing but inwardly are ravenous wolves".

Instead, The Handmaid's Tale explores how religion is used and abused – a classic example of life imitating art and art imitating life. For Atwood, the current crusade in the USA is less about religion and more about power, which explains why the words of Jesus, often preaching tolerance, have been disregarded.

"A lot of things that people cooked up and said were Christianity are not justified by the actual text," said Atwood. "If Christianity is a religion of love, what's all this other stuff going on, because it certainly looks an awful lot

like hate to me?"

Atwood wrote The Handmaid's Tale in the 1980s, just as the religious right were starting to ferment as a political force.

"Instead of just denouncing people and saying 'You're going to fry in hell', they mobilised," she said of that moment.

This perhaps explains why religious factions are more powerful at a time when people are less religious. According to a Gallup study, two-thirds of Americans born before 1946 belonged to a religious institution. Today, only 36% of millennials identify as religious. In a way this might be part of the problem. People stopped taking religion seriously. As Atwood said when asked how the religious right became so influential: "It's because those in the middle lost interest and didn't hold the middle ground so it allowed these things to be taken over." The middle ground would be a much more reasonable form of Christianity – one more consistent with the teachings of Jesus.

"I have studied the Bible and, in particular, the history of Israel, and at times when Israel has less power and has had to negotiate with its neighbours it was more tolerant. And at times when it had more power it became less tolerant," she said of another place currently on its knees because of the religious right.

"[Israel is] becoming less tolerant because the less tolerant factions within it have gained more power and do not have to negotiate as much as if they had less power."

Back in the USA, another reason that might explain the gains of the religious right lies with the left. Atwood is a firm advocate of free expression and has spoken out against cancel culture and restrictions on debate in modern culture.

With excitement, Atwood tells me

about a graph she has created. There is chaos at the bottom, totalitarianism at the top, the middle liberal democracy and arrows up and down on either side. Those who want power on the left and the right will both try to create chaos and will use whatever tools at their disposal, because that gives them a shot at totalitarianism.

"Shutting down speech on the left is just playing into this kind of scenario, and it's also a truism that any weapon that you devise – if it's an effective weapon – will be used against you," she said. "[Saying] you have to shut up and not say anything because you're hurting my feelings was done first on the left, but now it's being done in all of these states that are banning books on the right. 'You're hurting my feefees and therefore we're banning this book.'

"People who are actually interested in free speech have to realise that they cannot just defend the speech which they approve of. Free speech does mean free speech. There are always limits to it so you can't say 'Sign up here to become a child molester', but you have to defend the principle and a lot of people find it difficult to defend the right of their ideological enemies to express those opinions."

Atwood describes herself as a "modified optimist" ("I don't see any point in being a pessimist because then nobody does anything") and takes pride in being on the list of the most banned authors. What would she say to her censor? Her response is jocular.

"Thanks for increasing my sales!" she remarked, with a wry laugh. As she points out, her books are still readily available in shops – for now. ✖

Jemimah Steinfeld is editor-in-chief of Index

52(03):52/53|DOI: 10.1177/03064220231201296

King David he is not

Donald Trump has aligned himself with a religious right faction who see in him their saviour. If only they cared about rights. **JP O'MALLEY** speaks to **KATHERINE STEWART** about how we got here and what's next

KATHERINE STEWART BEGAN documenting the rise of the religious right more than a decade ago. Stewart's book, The Good News Club (2012), borrowed its title from an after-school Bible study programme with the same name.

"It describes itself as 'non-denominational', but it's highly sectarian and teaches children they can burn for an eternity if they fail to conform to a strict interpretation of the Christian faith," she told Index from her home in New York.

The journalist and bestselling author notes that in 2017 the administration of US president Donald Trump, using the term "school choice movement", allocated $1.4 billion of public funding to promote charter schools. "These are often run by people with covert religious or right-wing ideological agendas," Stewart explained.

In her more recent book, The Power Worshipers: Inside the Dangerous Rise of Religious Nationalism, she provides a detailed analysis of how US taxpayers' money is being used to promote far-right religious ideology in politics, education, schools, hospitals, civic spaces, courts, and both local and national communities.

The book begins by defining the American Christian nationalist movement. Today, Stewart elaborates on that definition. "It is radically anti-democratic because it claims that the foundation of legitimate

government in the USA is a strict interpretation of [Christianity] rather than our constitution, our representative government or the ideals of justice and equality that the American promise consists of," she said.

Made up of evangelical Christians, Protestants, ultra-conservative Catholics and some Pentecostalists, the American Christian nationalist movement is united by a common political vision, said Stewart. "This is not a culture war. The movement is ultimately trying to achieve political power and it now determines the future of the Republican Party."

In 2016, America's religious right got its first taste of power after Trump was elected as the 45th president of the USA. He promised his radically-religious-right voting base that he would appoint "pro-life" judges who would seek to end abortion rights, funnel public money to religious schools and enact far-right economic policies that many of the movement's plutocratic funders support.

"Trump largely delivered on those promises," Stewart said, adding that by the spring of 2018 there were weekly Bible study gatherings taking place at the White House. Some reportedly were held in the West Wing, and up to 11 of 15 cabinet secretaries, including then vice-president Mike Pence and education secretary Betsy DeVos, counted as participating members.

How has the religious right managed to gain such a strong

foothold in Washington? Just follow the money, says Stewart. She mentions organisations such as the Alliance Defending Freedom, an organisation that has an annual revenue of more than $50 million, which directs its efforts to dismantling the wall of separation between church and state. Stewart also speaks about the Federalist Society and the National Christian Foundation. The latter organisation is a "donor advised fund" that reportedly raised more than $1.5 billion in 2017.

Much of that funding has been channelled into highly sophisticated ways to mobilise a large voting base. Take, for example, United in Purpose: a non-profit organisation whose main mission is to unite like-minded conservative organisations in their quest to create a US society that is based entirely on Judeo-Christian principles.

"United in Purpose is now in a position to select the targets for its messaging from almost the entire voting-age population of the United States," said Stewart. "It begins by assigning points to each individual in its database for characteristics that line up with conservative religious voting patterns."

The religious right also plays a pivotal role in shaping how US healthcare facilities are run, she said. At the moment, an estimated one in six hospital beds in the USA is at a Catholic-run medical facility. Most are governed by Ethical and Religious Directives (these strict guidelines take moral instruction directly from the Vatican) and impose limitations on the types of services and procedures hospitals are able to deliver. To illustrate how dangerous this can be, Stewart cites an example from her book. It involved a doctor working in a Catholic-affiliated hospital in the USA not being able to prescribe birth control pills to a young woman with HIV. The patient was taking efavirenz, a potent anti-viral medication that can cause severe harm to a developing foetus, and subsequently ended up getting pregnant and giving

≡ **By the spring of 2018 there were weekly**
≡ **Bible study gatherings at the White House**

birth to a baby without a brain.

It's not an isolated incident, Stewart explains, adding: "The rate of maternal mortality in the United States is already the highest in the developed world, and it's sharply trending upward."

Stewart concludes by looking at what she claims is the Trump administration's most damaging legacy: the radical overhaul to the USA's judicial system.

By March 2019, 86 Trump judicial nominees had been confirmed since his inauguration – two to the Supreme Court, 31 to courts of appeal, and 53 to district and speciality courts. Trump also nominated 58 people to the federal courts during that timeframe. And she said key players from the USA's Christian nationalist movement helped advise Trump when and where those judicial appointments should occur.

In June 2022, two years into President Joe Biden's administration, the religious right achieved what is undoubtedly its greatest legal and moral victory to date, when Roe v Wade was overturned.

Since 1973, that Supreme Court ruling had held that the specific guarantee of "liberty" in the 14th Amendment of the US Constitution, which protects individual privacy, included the right to abortion prior to foetal viability – thus granting women abortion as a constitutional right.

"Even as it seeks to end abortion nationwide, along with emergency contraception and some widely practised forms of birth control, the Republican Party – which is beholden to America's religious right and relies on it for votes – is now an anti-family party that has somehow, by cloaking itself in the rhetoric of 'family values', passed itself off as pro-family," said Stewart.

Is there a pushback from either secular liberals or moderate conservatives? The rule of law and the separation of church and state is crucially important if US democracy is to survive; and Stewart said: "There are many legal advocacy groups committed to protecting individual rights, freedom

ABOVE: Former president Donald Trump poses with a Bible outside St. John's Episcopal Church in Washington DC, June 2020

of speech and conscience, and the separation of church and state, working in opposition to right-wing legal advocacy groups.

"There's a growing awareness that what we are dealing with here is a political movement, so awareness is a critical first step. As a journalist it is not my role to tell people how they should personally get involved in [taking on the religious right]. But there are no shortages of avenues for engagement. Whatever your lane, there are plenty of activists out there offering strategies and guidance. There is certainly a lot of work to be done, but for now we are free to do it."

But will radical US voters have the final say? Recent polls suggest that twice-indicted former president Trump leads across nearly every category and region, as voters seem to disregard any moral concerns about his escalating legal jeopardy. Stewart claims the

more Trump holds the rule of law in contempt, the more the religious right embraces his authoritarian values.

"Trump's clear disdain for the rules is part of his appeal," she said. "His transparently immoral character makes him the ideal leader of a religious nationalist state. Trump puts himself above the law, and is therefore representative of the authoritarian impulses of large numbers of his supporters who do not believe in equality or pluralism."

Stewart concluded: "They have made this explicit by comparing him to biblical figures like King David and King Cyrus.

"Trump is cast as an imperfect vessel whom God chose to enact His will and restore America to its 'Judeo-Christian' roots. If you believe you are in an existential struggle between absolute good and absolute evil, and you are fighting for your tribe, you don't want the nice guy who follows the rules." ✖

JP O'Malley is a British freelance journalist

52(03):54/55|DOI:10.1177/03064220231201300

No sex please, we're Hindus

Under India's far-right Bharatiya Janata Party, the definition of offence to Hindus has hugely expanded. The victims are numerous, says **SALIL TRIPATHI**

WHEN CHRISTOPHER NOLAN'S blockbuster film Oppenheimer opened around the world in July, it led to many spirited debates: about the ethics of using nuclear weapons to target civilians; the single-minded devotion with which scientists pursue a task, disregarding consequences; the witch-hunt against suspected communists in 1950s USA; and the director's aesthetic choices, such as not showing the devastation in Hiroshima and Nagasaki.

In India, the film became controversial for an entirely different reason. During a scene of ritualistic love-making between the scientist J Robert Oppenheimer and his lover, Jean Tatlock, he tries to impress her saying something arcane, and she challenges him to read a passage from another book, in a script that's foreign to her. She has picked the Bhagavad Gita, a long poem within the Sanskrit epic Mahabharata, where a reluctant Pandava prince Arjuna is encouraged by his charioteer, the Hindu god Krishna, to disregard his moral qualms and inhibitions, and plunge himself into the battle against evil, represented by Arjuna's cousins, Kauravas. The verse Oppenheimer recites, while unclothed, as Tatlock has mounted him, is: I am Death, the destroyer of all worlds.

There is a fascinating debate to be had about whether the word in that verse is "death" or "time", since in the original Sanskrit the word is, indeed, *kaala* or time. But the reason Hindu nationalists got apoplectic over the scene was not about the correct translation of that word; rather, they insisted, Hinduism was denigrated, since a holy phrase was uttered during a vulgar act.

This was preposterous on several levels; Hindu philosophy does not consider sex to be dirty or vulgar – temples in Konarak and Khajuraho have erotic sculptures that would require parental guidance. Sanskrit literature abounds with voyeuristic passages and celebrations of love and sex. But Uday Mahurkar, the self-styled founder of the so-called Save Culture Save India Foundation (he also happens to have the distinctly Orwellian job title of information commissioner of the government of India), wrote a blistering letter criticising the filmmaker for "a scathing attack on Hinduism".

He described the Gita as "a divine gift to human civilisation", which has inspired countless people to live a life of self-control and perform selfless noble deeds. He asked how India's Central Board of Film Certification approved the scene, which was "morally inappropriate, even disgusting". Such puritanical disgust for sex is, arguably, a Victorian imposition on Indian civilisation, given the lavish descriptions of sex in ancient scriptures, but then Hindu nationalists are not known for having homegrown wisdom.

For me, the drama over Oppenheimer brought a sense of déjà vu. In 1999, in Stanley Kubrick's film Eyes Wide Shut, during an orgy scene Sanskrit hymns are played in the background. Then, too,

> Militant Hindus personified the worst traits of other faiths they claimed to abhor

Hindus had fulminated, shouting: "No sex please, we're Hindus."

From the mid-1990s, for nearly a decade, I wrote a few pieces for Index in which I noted the rise of Hindu nationalists, who had begun challenging representations of Hindu culture and society by Indian and Western artists and scholars, initially in a comical manner but, over time, more viciously.

In 2009, I published my first book, Offence: The Hindu Case, as part of the Seagull Books series Manifestos for the 21st Century, in association with Index. In the book I outlined the outrage Hindu nationalists had shown for high art (such as the canvases of the late MF Husain), serious literature (such as the works of historian Romila Thapar) and popular entertainment (such as the Kubrick film or the singer Madonna performing while sporting a bindi on her forehead). Hindu nationalists were objecting to all forms of representation of Hindu culture that they believed undermined or denigrated Hinduism, turning a lively, inclusive, polytheistic, vibrant faith which had room for many gods as well as for atheism into a humourless, straitlaced, strict order, which would impose the idea of a singular god (Rama), a single book (Ramayana) and a single place of worship (Ayodhya).

That was the rationale behind the razing of the 16th-century mosque Babri Masjid in Ayodhya in 1992. The nationalists burned effigies, if not books, but later they burned people in the worst carnage India had known since independence from Britain in 1947, the pogrom in Gujarat in 2002.

Claiming to be adherents of a tolerant faith, militant Hindus personified the worst traits of other faiths they claimed

to abhor. They imitated their practices, including ostracising artists and calling for boycotts (as they have done to several Muslim movie stars in India in recent years); seeking bans on critical works (Bombay University removed Rohinton Mistry's novel Such A Long Journey, and India's ruling Bharatiya Janata Party's youth wing successfully campaigned against Paula Richman's book, Many Ramayanas, for carrying an essay offering alternative narratives of the Sanskrit epic that many Hindus revere, by vandalising a university campus); and murdering those who wrote critically of Hindu nationalism or Hindu superstition, including the rationalist Narendra Dabholkar in 2013, communist activist and writer Govind

Pansare in 2015, Kannada scholar MM Kalburgi in 2015 and the Kannada journalist Gauri Lankesh in 2017.

When Offence: The Hindu Case was published, a few liberal critics in India received it well, and a few Western academics engaged with it meaningfully, even when some of them were sceptical about my prognosis. My last paragraph read:

Whenever Hindu nationalists attack an art gallery, or tear down posters they consider obscene, or demand bans on books they don't want others to read, or vandalize a research institute, or destroy the home of an editor, or threaten an academic, or run a campaign against a historian they disagree with, or force film studios to change scripts, alter

ABOVE: Activists from Bharatiya Janata Yuva Morcha burn an effigy of Pakistani Foreign Minister Bilawal Bhutto Zardari following his remarks condemning treatment of Muslims under Modi, in Srinagar, Kashmir, December 2022

lyrics, or extract apologies from artists, or hurl eggs at scholars, or destroy mosques, rape Muslim women or kill Muslim men and children, they take India into a deeper abyss; they push Hinduism into a darker age. They look and act like the Nazis and the Taliban. They plunge their country into an area of darkness, are untrue to the meaning of their faith and are disloyal to their nation's constitution. They shame a great nation and belittle how Salman Rushdie saw India: "The dream we   →

→ had all agreed to dream."

One reviewer called my conclusions alarmist. Looking at the state of India now, I fear I might have underestimated what Hindu nationalists are capable of. Today, India is governed by its most out-and-out Hindu nationalist government, which has jailed more than 200 human rights defenders and activists, including scholars and writers. Most haven't been charged (and some are getting bail only after unconscionably long periods of delay), with states in India burning with fury over sectarianism, mosques razed, Muslim homes bulldozed, Muslims suspected of carrying beef (or storing beef at home) lynched, Muslims not allowed to pray in public, Muslim women and girls prohibited from wearing the hijab in some states, interfaith marriages made more difficult, hundreds of churches being burned, the sale of meat banned arbitrarily.

During certain Hindu festivals, processions of trident and sword-wielding angry men wearing saffron scarves march through areas where Muslims live and loudly taunt Muslims, and Muslims find

BELOW: Devotees visit the idol of Hindu god Khatu Shyam Baba, in the form of Lord Krishna, decorated with red tomatoes at a temple in Beawar, India. Hinduism is being placed centre stage in the country under Modi

it hard to buy or rent property.

India has violated the spirit of the UN Refugee Convention by declaring that from its immediate neighbourhood (Pakistan, Bangladesh and Afghanistan) it will let in only those asylum seekers as priority who are from minority faiths, essentially ruling out Muslims (see p.44 on the treatment of Rohingyas in Delhi). That means that Muslims in those countries who are LGBT+, women's rights activists, trade union leaders, or Sufis, Shias, Ahmedis or other minorities within Islam would not qualify, even though those communities sometimes face greater threats than Sikhs, Buddhists or Jains. (As an aside, Hindus in those countries do face discrimination and their rights are often violated.)

But discriminating among refugees is not permitted under the Refugee Convention. True, India hasn't signed the convention, but it had agreed to abide by its spirit in the past, in the years before Prime Minister Narendra Modi came to power, when India had taken in refugees from Tibet, Afghanistan, Sri Lanka, Myanmar and Bangladesh without checking their religion.

The US Commission on International Religious Freedom and the UK prime minister's special envoy for freedom of religion and belief have raised concerns over the situation in India and over the

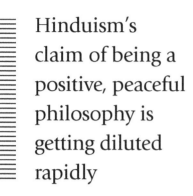

Hinduism's claim of being a positive, peaceful philosophy is getting diluted rapidly

treatment of its minorities. Soon after Modi left the USA after a triumphant visit to the White House, former US president Barack Obama expressed concern over how India was treating its minorities. Angry politicians from India's ruling party harshly criticised Obama in turn.

Hinduism's claim of being a positive, peaceful philosophy – thanks to the soft power of yoga, the outward charm of meditation, the fragrance of incense, the magnificent architecture of its temples, the evocative compassion for plants and animals in its literature, the beauty of the language of many of its scriptures and the popularity of some of its thinkers in the West, from Vivekananda in the 1890s to Maharishi Mahesh Yogi (who charmed The Beatles in the 1960s) – is getting diluted rapidly, as those claiming to speak in its name are imitating the worst traits of other religions over which they claim superiority.

When I completed Offence: The Hindu Case, I wanted to be optimistic, believing that this shall pass and, in what is now the world's most populous country, that the majority faith will live up to its claims and respect the dignity of other faiths and those with no faith. If I were to write a sequel, it would be much darker in its tone, as vociferous adherents of the faith want to become Death, destroyer of the world. ✖

Salil Tripathi is Index's contributing editor for South Asia

52(03):56/58|DOI:10.1177/03064220231201301

In the name of the father?

The last 12 months have seen escalating crackdowns – including executions – in the name of punishing those who offend the almighty, as shown in these examples alone by **FRANCIS CLARKE**

Iran

Two men were hanged in May after being charged by authorities with blasphemy. Yusef Mehrdad and Sadrullah Fazeli Zare were convicted of being members of a Telegram channel called Critique of Superstition and Religion.

Both men went on hunger strike in February 2022 after being denied family visits. Although death sentences are rare for blasphemy in Iran, they were part of a wave of executions across the country following months of unrest after the death of Jina "Mahsa" Amini last year.

Myanmar

Buddhist monks in Myanmar criticised the ruling Junta after they arrested a Swiss director and 13 amateur actors (including a 12-year-old) on the grounds that their movie blasphemes Buddhism. Don't Expect Anything was uploaded to the YouTube channel Isi Dhamma on 24 July, after which the regime vowed to take action against those involved for insulting the virtue of Buddhist monks and the country's traditions. Several monks though say the charge goes against Buddhist values of tolerance.

Indonesia

The decision by an elderly Muslim cleric to allow women and men to pray together in West Java sparked a backlash and resulted in charges of blasphemy being brought against him in August.

Panji Gumilang, 77, runs the Al-Zaytun boarding school in the district of Indramayu. The school previously faced backlash over its "unorthodox" practices, such as allowing women to become imams. In June, Indonesia's Islamic Clerical Council said it was investigating the school for "misguided religious practices". If found guilty of the charges, Gumilang faces up to 10 years in prison. Historically, Indonesia has practiced a tolerant form of Islam. However, there has been a rise in religious conservatism in recent years.

Pakistan

In April, a Chinese national was charged with blasphemy in Abbottabad. The engineer, identified only by the name Tian, was reportedly accused of insulting the Prophet Muhammed after he criticised two workers for taking too much time to pray on a break at the Dasu Dam Project.

Pakistan is a country where foreigners are rarely arrested for the crime, but around 400 locals gathered to protest and blocked a key highway before he was arrested. Tian was released from a high-security prison later that month after a court granted him bail, and it's unclear if he faced trial in Pakistan or if he was sent back to China.

Mauritania

A high school student was arrested in the town of Atar in July, accused of blasphemy, but her family is asking for forgiveness, saying she suffers from mental health issues. The unnamed girl was charged with disrespecting the Prophet Muhammed and using social networks "to undermine [the] holy values of Islam".

Mauritania has strengthened its blasphemy laws recently, removing a clause allowing offenders to escape the death sentence if they show remorse. The student could therefore face execution, after a period of no executions for blasphemy for 30 years.

Sweden/Iraq

In July, Iraq expelled Sweden's ambassador while protesters stormed its embassy in Baghdad and set fire to parts of the building. It was in response to the actions of Salwan Momika, a 37-year-old Iraqi refugee living in Sweden, who burned pages of the Koran outside the Iraqi embassy in Stockholm.

Several other protests occurred in Muslim-majority countries as governments in Iraq, Turkey, the United Arab Emirates, Jordan and Morocco condemned the incident as both blasphemous and Islamophobic. Sweden abolished blasphemy laws in 1970 and some have argued for their return, but others have said that both protesting and the burning of books is an important part of the right to free expression.

Poland

In a rare positive example, the European Court of Human Rights ruled in September 2022 that a pop star convicted of blasphemy 10 years earlier had had her rights violated. Dorota Rabczewska, whose stage name is Doda, was fined 5,000 zloty (around $1,200) by a court in Warsaw in 2012 for saying she was more convinced by dinosaurs than the Bible, and those who wrote the Bible took drugs and drank too much wine.

The court in Strasbourg ruled that her comments were protected by her right to free speech. The court ordered the Polish authorities to pay Doda €10,000 ($10,800) – nine times the amount of her original fine. ✖

Francis Clarke is editorial assistant at Index

52(03):59/59|DOI:10.1177/03064220231201304

A call to harm

Pakistan has some of the world's harshest blasphemy laws, and the punishments are often handed out by violent mobs, writes **AYESHA KHAN**

ABOVE: A demonstrater protests the Supreme Court decision to overturn the conviction of Asia Bibi on 2 November 2018 in Lahore, Pakistan. Bibi is a Christian woman who spent eight years on death row after a dispute with neighbours resulted in her being accused of blasphemy. The decision triggered violent protests by religious hardliners

N A VILLAGE near Sargodha, in Pakistan, Haroon Shehzad was arrested after a Muslim neighbour called for charges of blasphemy against him based on a Facebook post. Shehzad, who is Christian, had posted verses from the Bible about food sacrificed to idols on 30 June this year, which his fellow townsman, Muhammad Imran Ullah, took as an attack on Eid al-Adha, the Islamic festival of sacrifice. The post itself made no direct mention of the festival.

Screenshots of the post circulated locally, but tensions increased when the local mosque made announcements asking people to protest, leading

many Christian families to flee in fear. Members of Shehzad's family also had to hide because even the initial protests caused them to fear for their lives. Shehzad was granted pre-arrest bail, but held in "protective custody". At his bail hearing, which he was not allowed to attend, people shouted slogans in the courtroom and warned Shehzad's lawyers that they might be attacked.

Shehzad's case is one of many, and accusations of blasphemy under Pakistan's penal code are punishable by imprisonment, fines and even death. With accusations under this law increasing, Shehzad risks being just another number among the lives threatened and lost to lynching, mob violence and years of court proceedings.

In August 2023, lawmakers passed

 If you cannot define disrespect, any action can be constituted as disrespect

changes to blasphemy laws which will increase the scope and punishments, with possible life sentences for anyone who insults companions and wives of the Prophet Muhammad. It put the issue in the spotlight once again, but even when there's no media attention, this is an issue that never goes away.

"This isn't something that has happened recently. The embeddedness of religion and influence of religious leaders in our daily life in Pakistan is so high," said development worker Elaine Alam. And while lawmakers cited this change as a way to stop misuse of the law, Alam doesn't believe that to be accurate.

"In Pakistan's case, the effect on public understanding [of the law] is a very dangerous one," she said. As seen in Shehzad's situation and the hundreds of cases before his, people take the law into their own hands long before the legal system gets a chance.

As part of the country's penal code, clauses were added to existing laws between 1980 and 1986 that detailed a series of different offences – from disturbing religious rituals and disrespect against the Prophet to other categories of insult or derogatory remarks.

Data from the National Commission for Justice and Peace shows that between 1987 and 2018, 776 Muslims, 505 Ahmedis, 229 Christians and 30 Hindus were accused of blasphemy. More concerning trends associated with these accusations are the lynchings and mob violence that have become a common reaction by the public.

Noman Masih, a 22-year-old Christian from Bahawalpur, was sentenced to death on 30 May – four years after his arrest. Lazar Allah Rakha, Masih's lawyer, has been a human rights defender for more than 20 years. He told Index, in response to the outcome of Masih's case: "There was no proof, and it was clear there was a lot of pressure as the judge waited five months after the hearing to announce the verdict."

Legal analyst and researcher Peter Jacob, the executive director of the

 # The damage caused by these laws runs far deeper than just the verdicts

Pakistan-based research and advocacy organisation Centre for Social Justice, has been working on issues related to the blasphemy laws since the 1990s. He said that he's observed how these laws are used to accuse more Muslims than minority groups, but that the first resulting death by lynching was of a Christian teacher.

Speaking of the law, he said: "It's a unique example because there isn't, in modern times, any legislation which criminalises certain presupposed acts, so there's a problem with the text, not only the use. The text itself is creating space for misuse and massive abuse.

"The law fails to define what respect is. If you cannot define disrespect, any action can be constituted as disrespect when law itself is neutral. As long as it stays like this, it's a ground for people to create an infrastructure of hatred and it'll create a demand for victims."

Jacob's words come from decades of observing the use of the law and its impact on social structure and power dynamics. Allah Rakha has noticed similar trends in his law practice. He said that, while he feels a responsibility to take these cases, other lawyers are too afraid to associate with the issues. He often observes how the accused lose so much of their lives, even when acquitted. The damage caused by these laws runs far deeper than just the verdicts.

"There's the case of Mohammad Asif, which has been going on for 10 years and yet not even one witness has been allowed. Multiple lawyers came and left that case, and he's spent 10 years in jail despite the medical board filing a report saying he is medically insane," Allah Rakha said.

He references numerous other cases and points out that despite not one person actually being hanged for a blasphemy offence, lives are ruined every day. He's seen families having to go

underground, and had cases where the accused is ostracised from society long before the court reaches its verdict.

Much of his aim with his work has been to show the country's Muslim majority that non-Muslims are law-abiding citizens, just as they are. But laws such as this make that difficult because it becomes easy to paint a target on anyone's back.

Farah Zia, director of the Human Rights Commission of Pakistan, points out that "blasphemy laws are often misused to settle personal scores, or to grab property — because the threshold of evidence is very low".

Activists also highlight that the government has a large role to play in exacerbating this issue, not only in creating the laws but also in turning a blind eye to escalating situations.

"There has to be an acknowledgement at the parliamentary level that abuse is happening. The government doesn't admit the law has any problem," said Jacob. "Our society is held hostage to a mindset that's taken a deep root in our society and now the government wants to avoid the issue which has aggravated the situation. Four people have been lynched and there have been 70 cases this year alone."

Decades of ignoring the issue have created a deep-set rot, and the result is a violent reaction from mobs at the mere hint of an accusation.

"There's no solution except education," Alam said. "Education which helps you critically analyse, helps you put others first [and] helps you understand civil liberties and what exactly nationalism is, because it's not just faith." ✖

Ayesha Khan is a journalist based in Pakistan

52(03):60/61 | DOI:10.1177/03064220231201305

The blasphemy obstacle course

With her novel inspired by Kuwait's dealings with blasphemy laws,
MAI AL-NAKIB explores how the climate can lead to self-censorship

CREDIT: Yasser Al-Zayyat/AFP via Getty

FREEDOM OF EXPRESSION, opinion, religion, research and publication is constitutionally guaranteed in Kuwait, as long as it is "in accordance with the conditions specified by law".

Numerous laws and amendments restrict these guarantees. They include potential prison terms or fines for speech and publications or online content that criticises the emir or regional leaders; disparages the constitution, public prosecutors or judiciary; threatens national unity and security; incites violence; or is treasonous. While there is no distinct blasphemy law, restrictions are embedded within various laws – namely, defaming Islam, Christianity or Judaism; inciting sectarian violence; and insulting the Quran, God or the prophet Muhammad and his wives.

Reading over these convoluted laws is sobering. They possess an element of ambiguity that allows them to be stretched to serve political or social interests. The cascade of amendments forms a net, potentially trapping those who have no intention of crossing any lines. This state of affairs breeds fear, which often results in self-censorship. Writers, journalists, academics and activists bear the brunt of censorial scrutiny, but a generalised dread inevitably trickles down to all citizens and residents, stifling expression and the possibility of a genuinely tolerant, civil and open society.

In 2013, Kuwait's parliament passed an amendment to the 2012 National Unity Law, making blasphemy a capital crime. The government ultimately did not approve that decision. Nonetheless, the fact that a parliamentary majority would consider blasphemy worth condemning people to death over was an unprecedented development. While Kuwait practises capital punishment in rare cases, it is usually reserved for murder, drug trafficking or child molestation – never for anti-religious expression.

All this had a chilling effect on me as a writer and a teacher, although I did not allow it to curb my work. It ended up informing the plot of my novel, An Unlasting Home, in which the protagonist, Sara al-Ameed, professor of philosophy at Kuwait University, is accused of blasphemy and threatened with execution if convicted.

In 2014, I was up for promotion from assistant to associate professor at the university. My file included an article that proposed an "ethics of the missing" as a way to reckon with the disturbing aftermath of what befell the Palestinian community in Kuwait after its liberation in 1991. I was strongly urged by the chair of the departmental promotions committee to withdraw the article because it was politically controversial and not sufficiently literary. It became clear that even though the article was published by a peer-reviewed international journal in my academic field, I would not be promoted if I insisted on submitting it.

I decided to withdraw the article and replace it with another about Palestinian writer Ghassan Kanafani, which engaged similar issues but through literature. I secured my promotion.

In 2018, my collection of short stories, The Hidden Light of Objects, was banned along with more than 4,500 other books by a 12-member censorship committee in the Ministry of Information. The law that resulted in these sweeping bans was

 Kuwait's parliament passed an amendment to the 2012 National Unity Law, making blasphemy a capital crime

ABOVE: Books hang from trees outside the
National Assembly building in Kuwait City in
September 2018 in protest against the government's
censorship regulations on publications

amended by parliament in 2020 thanks to activist pressure. While certainly a positive development, it did not resolve the problem altogether since publications remain subject to the censorship laws mentioned above, leaving writers, publishers and distributors vulnerable to receiving legal action.

My reaction to the university episode was rage. My reaction to my book being banned was exhaustion. I decided not to take either case to constitutional court, which I had every right to do. My decision could be interpreted as a form of self-censorship: by not actively challenging the powers that be, I was compounding the problem. But not everyone is made for

legal wrangling. Court cases can take years and, in the process, take years off the lives of those of us with a low tolerance for bureaucratic absurdities. My choice not to contest the censorship enabled me to use my time to complete An Unlasting Home.

I write in English and publish outside Kuwait, so I did not have to consider how my novel would be received locally. Many writers, academics and artists in Kuwait take this route.

Rather than viewing this as self-censorship, I regard it as a form of cultural resistance with ramifications inside the country. Nothing can be hidden anymore. Culture moves along electronic circuits from the outside

in, countering censorship in ways authorities cannot control. These cultural expressions are intransigent in the best possible sense, engaging the present while preparing the conditions for an alternative future – one in which censorship is no longer an obstacle.

Mai al-Nakib is an author and associate professor of English and comparative literature at Kuwait University

52(03):62/63|DOI:10.1177/03064220231201307

Self-worship is the new religion

TARA ISABELLA BURTON explores the USA's new, customisable "religion", which comes with its own form of blasphemy

CREDIT: Everett Collection Inc / Alamy

LAST MONTH, I met a group of people who believe that human beings have it all figured out – or, at least, that we very soon will.

I'd been invited to give a lecture on a conference cruise called Summit at Sea. Most of the participants were drawn from the start-up, tech and wellness worlds. What they shared was a passion for combining the technological and the religious – "hacking" our brains and souls alike in the service of personal growth and human potential.

Panels on sexual-somatic healing and psychedelics for self-improvement alternated with more traditional talks on artificial intelligence and machine learning. Our cabin gift bags were replete with nootropics (or "smart drugs"), each claiming to better our cognitive, emotional or sexual health. Participants pitched one another (and sometimes me) ideas for start-ups that almost invariably involved paths towards what they saw as personal and spiritual self-actualisation. One woman intended to sell bath products associated with cleansing, purification and other elements of traditional African folk magic. Another planned a start-up connecting busy professionals with high-level spiritual practitioners in fields ranging from trauma healing to psychedelic coaching.

In an era when fewer Americans identify as traditionally religious — about a quarter of Americans and a third of millennials and members of generation Z identify as religiously unaffiliated — the religious landscape has shifted. Spirituality is increasingly not something we do in a church or synagogue but something we carefully customise, curate and remix in accordance with our own personal sense of self-being.

In the wake of this shift, a vast and diverse "spiritual marketplace" has arisen to help the spiritual consumer find the products, classes and bespoke gathering spaces that are right for them – from femme-coded wellness gurus such as Goop founder Gwyneth Paltrow to masculinity influencers including Andrew Tate, and from witch-influencers to stoicism bloggers.

Central to this new ethos is the idea that the most important thing we can do is live an "authentic" life – one where the practices and pursuits feel that they are in accordance with our values and desires. By attending a Soulcycle class, optimising our productivity patterns through "life-hacking" tips and consuming nootropics or psychedelics to expand our minds or consciousnesses, we are expected to spend our leisure time and money on highly individualised journeys of personal growth.

But we have absorbed, too, that idea's troubling corollary that we have little or no obligation to those we do not choose – to our families, our communities or those vulnerable or marginalised people who, for whatever reason, have not managed to achieve the so-called "personal growth" we claim for ourselves.

The belief that we owe it to ourselves to "live our best lives", to be our "best selves" and to purchase the supplements, fitness classes, bullet journals, scented candles and bath supplies, has become inextricably intertwined with the modern American dream. So, too, has the conviction that, by turning inwards and focusing on our own goals and

If there is a sense of blasphemy in this new religion, it is in the notion that sometimes our feelings, our perceptions and our desires are, in fact, invalid

our own desires rather than those of the collective society around us, we can somehow harness the universe's "energy" to get what we want.

More than half of Americans now believe in manifesting: the quasi-magical notion that we can bring ourselves wealth, health or romantic success by believing hard enough in ourselves.

The gospel of "life-hacking" is largely an individualistic one – one that celebrates personal achievement and our focus on private feeling or experience at the expense of other elements of our humanity. There is little room in such an ideology to focus on the parts of human existence that we do not or cannot choose: the inevitability of our deaths, the proper way to respond to suffering or illness or loss, and the social relationships – familial and communal alike – that do not conform to our affinities or boundaries.

If there is a sense of blasphemy in this new religion, it is in the notion that sometimes our feelings, our perceptions and our desires are, in fact, invalid. The idea that something might feel authentic or meaningful to us but be morally or ethically wrong, or that our own innermost sense of self might diverge from obligations we have to other people or to the world at large, is virtually anathema.

During my time at the conference, I repeatedly found that self-denial – unless we were talking about intermittent fasting or other diet hacks – was looked on with suspicion. Almost unanimously, the wellness apps and start-up practices were designed to help users pursue the hyper-individualistic goals and desires they chose, rather than encouraging them to question what those goals and desires should be.

The liberating possibility of

ABOVE: A scene from an episode of The Goop Lab, a documentary series about the lifestyle and wellness company Goop, founded by American actress Gwyneth Paltrow

technology – which has allowed us to transcend so many of our physical and geographic limitations – has made us uncomfortable with the idea of limits at all. We are whoever we want to be.

But the human condition has always been one of balancing human freedom with human vulnerability – our ability to dream and desire with our status as social, animal beings who live in, and with, shared communities. It is a truth today's new religions refuse to acknowledge. ✖

Tara Isabella Burton is a novelist, writer and theologian and the former religion reporter for Vox

52(03):64/65|DOI:10.1177/03064220231201308

Think of the children

One of the most banned authors in the USA, **JUNO DAWSON**, talks to **KATIE DANCEY-DOWNS** about arriving at book talks for children accompanied by a bodyguard

ON THE US tour of her children's picture book You Need to Chill, Juno Dawson took a bodyguard. The book's front cover shows a curly-haired child wearing heart sunglasses, proclaiming it to be "a story of love and family," but the British author's US publishers were serious about safety.

"As it was, this poor security guard had the most blissed-out week of his life, given that it was just lovely children coming to hear me read a picture book," Dawson told Index. "But how sad that my publisher had to even think about hiring plainclothes security officers. I felt very Whitney Houston, living my Bodyguard fantasy."

She mocks her own gallows humour — ultimately, a children's author needed a bodyguard. Being a trans writer, she said, there is an ever-present threat. When she had the honour of opening a bookshop in Brighton the event also needed a bouncer.

Dawson not only holds the unenviable position of tied 10th place in the American Library Association's (ALA) top 10 most challenged books of 2022 with This Book is Gay, she's also a trans woman, an intersection which puts her at increased risk. The tour went to bookshops and conferences only, not to those most dangerous of places — schools and libraries. The threat is all too real. In March 2023, the Hilton school district in New York State was evacuated after receiving bomb threats over particular books, specifically naming Dawson's teen sex education book, This Book is Gay.

When the award-winning novelist, screenwriter and journalist faced her first book challenge, a censorship demand made to libraries and which can lead to a local ban, her friends in publishing told her she'd made it, that she'd arrived. But when Index asked her how it actually feels to be a banned author, she said: "The one-word answer is 'bad.'"

"You want your work to be out there and you want it to reach an audience. While there is that ego boost seeing your name in the papers and seeing your book cause controversy, at the same time, all I was really left with is [sadness] — how can it possibly be that in 2023 we're still having quite serious conversations about the existence of LGBTQ youth?"

Dawson went to school in the UK under the full force of Section 28, legislation brought in by the then Prime Minister Margaret Thatcher's government in 1988 which banned "promoting homosexuality" in schools and included teaching about "the acceptability of homosexuality as a pretended family relationship". Over three decades later and 20 years after the law was repealed, Dawson is astounded that "people are still trying to ban books about queer youth".

This Book is Gay deals with sex, same-sex sex and faith, which Dawson describes as a "triple whammy" and makes it a prime target for book challenges. She is clear that it's not just one faith group putting on pressure. The nonfiction book was first published in the USA in 2015, but has only recently made it onto the banned list.

"One of the key issues is people aren't actually reading the book. And so what happens is actually they are protesting books which have appeared on other lists," she said. "Vexatious people and groups who are trying to ban books are not going to books and reading books. They are just scouring the internet for books that they should be irate about."

Now that This Book is Gay has appeared on the ALA list, Dawson expects it will continue appearing for years to come, with the current list acting like "a shopping list for the far right to get worked up about".

Dawson's book sits alongside 1,647 others recorded by PEN America as being targeted in the 2021-22 school year, with the highest number of bans coming from Texas and Florida. A huge proportion of the challenged books deal with LGBTQ+ issues, with Maia Kobabe's Gender Queer and George M. Johnson's All Boys Aren't Blue topping the ALA list. Those discussing issues of race and racism are also targeted for bans.

The 2022 challenges are nearly double that of 2021 according to the ALA, and Dawson puts this down to the organisation of conservative groups. She highlights a new tactic which has sprung from the QAnon conspiracy

> This Book is Gay deals with sex, same-sex sex and faith, which Dawson describes as a "triple whammy" for what makes it a target for book challenges

CREDIT: Zefrog/Alamy

LEFT: YA author and trans activist Juno Dawson

theory movement: accusing those who support the teaching of LGBTQ+ issues in schools of being "groomers".

"I'd like to think in 2023 we've moved past the notion that LGBTQ people are somehow predatory," Dawson said.

She wants people to think about the consequences of banning books, particularly those people who attempt to score political points by doing so.

"Bigots never think they're being bigots," Dawson said. "They always say this is about concern: 'We're concerned about the children.' And what I would say is that concern isn't going to stop an LGBTQ+ child from being LGBTQ+. It's not a choice. It's not something anybody has any say over. But by removing these books, what you're doing is you're taking away support."

When she wrote This Book is

Gay, Dawson was thinking about her own experience in the 1990s, and how a lack of information left her unprepared, and even meant she got into dangerous situations.

"So when you come at me saying, 'Won't somebody think of the children?' I say 'Yeah, let's!' Let's think about those young queer people who, whether you like it or not, regardless of your faith, those people are going to be gay or bi or trans or non-binary, and you are taking help away from them."

In the UK, Dawson is a School Role Model for LGBTQ+ rights organisation Stonewall, and she has seen differences in how books like hers are treated in the two countries.

"We know you can go on 4chan or 8chan or Reddit and see a group discussing which book to challenge and how to go about challenging them.

And I think that was particularly after [President] Trump lost the election, and the Maga crowd refocused their efforts on a much more local grassroots level," she said. "I'm not sensing there is an appetite for that in the UK — yet. And that's a really big yet, because actually, far right groups in the UK do look to what's happening in America for inspiration."

She describes the huge influence of far-right groups like Libs of TikTok, which have not taken hold in the UK. But with an election year coming up in the UK and "the culture war in full swing" nothing is certain. While the UK might currently be spared from official book challenges, Dawson highlights that there is no equivalent to the ALA monitoring in the UK.

"It could be that my book is being removed from libraries left, right and centre actually, but we just don't know about it," she said. Research by the Chartered Institute of Library and Information Professionals in April 2023 found that a third of librarians in the UK have been asked by members of the public to remove books, and that the phenomenon is increasing.

"I had an invitation to visit a school rescinded and they wouldn't really provide an explanation, but it was all very mysterious. That was at a Catholic school," Dawson said.

There was a similar story for children's author Simon James Green in 2022, whose World Book Day visit to a Catholic school was cancelled, resulting in some of the teachers protesting. His book included gay characters.

When Dawson faces a book challenge in the USA, she is often the last to find out. Sometimes librarians ask for help directly when groups try to get her books removed from their schools, and at other times she hears from organisations like PEN America, the ALA and the National Coalition Against Censorship. On other →

Who's afraid of the big bad book?

The books that top the list of most frequently banned across the USA in 2022

Gender Queer: A Memoir by Maia Kobabe
A 2019 graphic memoir written and illustrated by Kobabe. It recounts Kobabe's journey from adolescence to adulthood and the author's exploration of gender identity and sexuality, before identifying as non-binary.

All Boys Aren't Blue by George M Johnson
A YA memoir that follows journalist and LGBTQ+ activist George M Johnson, it explores their childhood, adolescence and university years, growing up under the duality of being Black and queer.

The Bluest Eye by Toni Morrison
First published in 1970, Morrison's debut novel is an examination of the obsession with beauty and conformity, and asks questions about race, class and gender. The calls to ban the novel from schools and libraries started from the get-go.

Flamer by Mike Curato
Curato's debut graphic novel draws on his own experiences about the struggle of dealing with sexuality, race and gender as a young mixed-race boy while going to summer camp.

Looking for Alaska by John Green
A coming-of-age novel that touches on themes of grief, hope and youth-adult relationships. With complaints about language, sexual content and LGBTQ+ themes, it was 2015's most banned book.

The Perks of Being a Wallflower by Stephen Chbosky
A story centred around the character Charlie, an introverted and observant child, through his freshman year of high school in a Pittsburgh suburb. The book has frequently been on the banned list since publication in 1999 due to its sexual content, and alcohol and drugs references.

Lawn Boy by Jonathan Evison
A semi-autobiographical novel that tells the story of Mike Muñoz, who is trying to find his way economically, socially and sexually. Like others on the list, it covers sexual activities and LGBTQ+ themes. Evison has stated his novel wasn't meant for school libraries, and a spate of misinformation about paedophile content was spread regarding the book.

The Absolutely True Diary of a Part-Time Indian by Sherman Alexie
A novel that chronicles contemporary adolescence through the eyes of an Indigenous boy. It has been banned in some places in the past for references to masturbation and use of profanities.

Out of Darkness by Ashley Hope Perez
A historical YA novel, Out of Darkness chronicles a love affair between a Mexican-American girl and an African-American boy in 1930s New London, Texas. It has been banned in numerous school districts across the country on the basis of having sexually explicit passages and depicting abuse.

A Court of Mist and Fury by Sarah J. Maas
A Court of Mist and Fury was the subject of court action when a Virginia legislator tried to prevent the book chain Barnes and Noble from stocking it. The book has been described as having graphic sexual content.

Crank by Ellen Hopkins
Based loosely on the real-life addictions of the author's daughter to crystal meth, Crank has frequently been banned and challenged because of drugs, offensive language and sexually explicit content.

Me and Earl and the Dying Girl by Jesse Andrews
Described as a "weird little anti-romance about a teenage boy whose mom forces him to befriend a girl with cancer", the book has frequently been challenged due to accusations of profanity and sexual depiction.

This Book Is Gay by Juno Dawson
A non-fiction book described by Dawson as a "guidebook for young people discovering their sexual identity and how to navigate those uncomfortable waters," This Book is Gay is frequently targeted by right-wing groups since publication.

→ occasions, Dawson finds out about book challenges when she embarks on a sporadic google of herself.

"I feel much more strongly for the people who are on the front line, and that is usually librarians and educators," she said. With a history as a primary school teacher, she understands what it's like to stand at the school gate waving the class goodbye, only to see an incoming parent with a grievance. "It doesn't feel entirely safe."

Those people on the frontline often make it their mission to fight back.

"Almost as much as the books, it's about them being visible role models for the young people in their communities. Because let's be quite clear, when people challenge a book about race, or a book about being LGBTQ, really what they're trying to ban is being queer, or they're trying to restrict the lives of young Black people," she said. "Every time somebody steps into this sort of battle as an ally, it's to show those young people that there are still adults in their life who have got their back."

That's exactly why authors like Dawson are so vocal, why they speak up on social media and in interviews.

She works with PEN America and has cheered on as some of her US contemporaries sue a Florida school district over book bans. She believes the fight can happen on a number of fronts, and that even from her base in Brighton, there's an active role she can take: "I think there is a power in me remembering what my job is, which is to keep writing these books." ✖

Katie Dancey-Downs is assistant editor at Index

52(03):66/68|DOI: 10.1177/03064220231201309

Turkey's zealots still want blood

Aziz Nesin was caught in the middle of Turkey's anti-Salman Rushdie campaign in 1993. Thirty years on, extremist Muslims are attacking his foundation. **KAYA GENÇ** speaks to its current director about the situation

AMONG THE GLOBAL Islamist backlash against Salman Rushdie's novel The Satanic Verses in the late 1980s and the early 1990s, events in Turkey stood out. In terms of numbers, they resulted in the steepest death toll. On 2 July 1993, 37 intellectuals participating in a literary festival in the eastern Anatolian town of Sivas were burned to death by a mob of radical Islamists. The mob demanded that their target, Aziz Nesin, who had recently began translating The Satanic Verses into Turkish, be handed over so he could be executed. When Nesin's friends refused, Islamists set fire to the hotel where novelists, poets, scholars and others had taken refuge.

The spectre of this crime against humanity continues to haunt Turkey three decades on. Anyone associated with the legacy of Nesin – who died in 1995 – is viewed with suspicion in Islamist strongman Recep Tayyip Erdogan's "New Turkey".

Since 2020, the Nesin Foundation, established in 1973 as a boarding school with a capacity of 40 children in Istanbul's Çatalca neighbourhood, has been a target of Erdogan's regime. That year, the foundation fell out with Rabıta, an Islamist foundation linked to influential Islamic sect the İsmailağa, after Rabıta members moved in next door. In 2021, two Rabıta members, Sezar Korkmaz and his son Ahmet, attacked the foundation's director, Süleyman Cihangiroğlu, so violently that he had to go to hospital. Soon afterwards, Erdogan blocked the Nesin Foundation's accounts.

Members of Rabıta were undoubtedly aware of Aziz Nesin's progressive legacy when they attacked its director. Erdogan

was aware of it, too. As Istanbul's mayor in 1994, a year after the Sivas massacre, he said: "We'll excise Aziz Nesin's name from Istanbul's streets."

Just two months before the hotel was set alight, Nesin, a legendary humorist, had published portions of Rushdie's novel in Aydınlık, a leftist newspaper he edited. On 11 May, he penned an op-ed piece titled "The Satanic Verses will be published", and claimed: "I think that Turks, because they've Turkified Islam, won't murder in the name of religion. I might be wrong… But we can prove by publishing Rushdie's book that Turkey's true intellectuals will not stray from rationality, even under death threats."

Nesin's optimism didn't diminish after the government made its position on the Rushdie affair clear by outlawing the importing of The Satanic Verses into Turkey. It also banned any attempt to translate the text into Turkish.

On 28 May, Nesin addressed government ministers in an open letter. "If there are human rights in Turkey, if there is freedom of thought and religious belief in Turkey, how can you issue a decree that stops the novel The Satanic Verses from being imported to Turkey?" he asked.

Nesin's aim, in his words, was to ensure that "The Satanic Verses can be published in Turkey, as in all other civilised countries". He also made the issue a litmus test about whether Turkey was genuinely secular. In that test, Turkey failed: The Satanic Verses

remains unpublished in Turkish 34 years after its publication, even while the rest of Rushdie's bibliography is available for readers in a country that has been ostensibly secular since the 1920s.

But Nesin's test revealed something even more crucial. The hotel massacre, from which he emerged alive, exposed the true agenda of Turkey's Islamists to the public, raising doubts about their legitimacy.

In 1993, when Erdogan was the mayor, Nesin participated in a live television debate with the future strongman and claimed the Islamist would "erase all the names of people like me, once he achieves true power".

Cihangiroğlu knows about the violence of politics from his personal experience of 2021. His brother, Halit Güngen, was a journalist for the 2000'e Doğru magazine, in which he published an investigative report into the Islamic organisation Hizbollah's links with the Turkish government in 1992.

Two days after his piece came out, he was murdered in the magazine's office in Diyarbakır. A lifetime fan of Nesin's books, Güngen had penned a letter to his idol two years before his death and asked to be accepted to his foundation as a pupil.

"You have educated yourself; do you have a brother?" Nesin wrote back. So Güngen sent his 13-year-old brother, Süleyman, to Nesin in 1990.

Today, Cihangiroğlu runs the Nesin Foundation. In a recent interview, →

≡ The Satanic Verses remains unpublished in Turkish 34 years after its publication

Two days after his piece came out, he was murdered in the magazine's office

→ he said Islamist attacks against the foundation had increased in the 2020s.

On 28 May this year, the day Erdogan won a new term as Turkey's president, for example, Cihangiroğlu and his staff were shocked by the violent celebrations of their neighbours.

"They use each opportunity to abuse us," he said. "During the election night, they threw fireworks and used their guns to shoot in the air. Maybe they were not aware, but there are tall pine trees on the border of two buildings, and because they had directed their fireworks and guns at us, those might have caught fire. In that case, they'd have burnt their property and ours. Their abuse has reached a level of stupidity. What century are we living in? They've been firing guns in front of children as young as five. I hear, with my ears, the kids asking them whether those are blank cartridges. Their celebrations continued until the early hours of the next day."

When members of Rabıta moved next door to the Nesin Foundation in 2020, shortly after the Covid-19 outbreak began, Cihangiroğlu initially had no idea who they were. "They seemed like nice, elderly, bearded uncles," he said. "We never complained about their prayers. But one year after they moved, we started seeing busloads of children and adults coming and using a sound system at night for their prayers. Because we're so close geographically, the sounds they made at 11pm began to annoy us immensely."

When Cihangiroğlu complained, an administrator of Rabıta said they were exercising their freedom of religion. "And I said, 'Exercise it by all means, but please don't use the sound system at 11pm. We have small children at our foundation and staff members trying to sleep'." Elders from Rabıta later came to apologise. But in the following weeks, Cihangiroğlu started hearing

demonising rhetoric about the Nesin Foundation being disseminated by Rabıta members. "We've been here for 50 years. I've lived here for 30 years, first as a student and now as director. We know so many people in this area, and we heard from them that Rabıta members were saying things like, 'We're anti-Nesin people; we're waging war against the Nesin people. Support us in our cause'. Such talk is very dangerous. When we notified the mayor about this, we heard a lecture on democracy and how anyone should be able to pray as they liked."

Among the rumours Rabıta members spread was that the Nesin Foundation wasn't a single-sex school, which was against Islam. This inflammatory rhetoric brought back memories of the fundamentalists from the early 90s and their call to "burn Nesin the Satanic".

But Cihangiroğlu doesn't think Rabıta members took orders for their attacks from the top. "Theirs is more of a fool's courage," he said. "They keep on coming to us because nobody stops them."

After the initial conflict, an inspection team from the Directorate General for Relations with Civil Society knocked on Cihangiroğlu's door in 2022 and notified him that because they hadn't received permission for their donation campaigns, their accounts would be frozen. They were regular donations, although the authorities treated them as though they were campaign donations. But the reaction to the freezing of the accounts showed that the foundation's values were shared widely around the country. "People from nationalist, leftist and other political camps contacted us in solidarity and called this a big injustice," said Cihangiroğlu.

The raid was shocking for pupils of the foundation. "Inspectors entered female students' rooms and even tried

to look inside their drawers. As the foundation's director, I don't have the right to enter a child's room. When I go, I knock on the door and would never enter a room if I didn't hear a sound back. But these inspectors came and just rushed into the rooms."

The assaults of Erdogan's regime on

ABOVE: A woman holds a portrait during a march in Ankara on the 24th anniversary of the Sivas massacre on 2 July 2017. 37 people were killed after a mob arson attacked the Otel Madimak in the Turkish city

Nesin's legacy reminded many Turks of another strongman, Kenan Evren, who ruled Turkey with an iron fist between 1980 and 1989 and similarly despised Nesin. "After Kenan Evren instigated his coup in 1980, everyone suffered – from left to right – but Nesin was alone in his public rebellion," said Cihangiroğlu. "He published a Petition of Intellectuals against the dictator when everyone was terrified about whether Evren's junta may detain them. Nesin's was an unforgettable gesture. As with all good and beautiful things, that gesture remains relevant today."

Among Turkey's writers who grew up admiring Nesin's stubborn defence of freedom of expression is the novelist →

→ Burhan Sönmez. "Throughout his life, Aziz Nesin struggled to bring out the meaning of freedom and tell that to people," Sönmez said in an interview with Index. "Maybe he wasn't able to change Turkey. But he changed me and many others like me. He raised us, and he made us believe in freedom. I think this was his victory. Even if we can't change the system, transforming one person and believing in the future is a victory. When he was drafting the Petition of Intellectuals and publishing The Satanic Verses, despite all the threats, Nesin's aim was not to beat the system. He knew he'd fail in that. He wanted to keep the passion for freedom fresh in people."

As director of PEN International since 2021, Sönmez has been reminding people of Nesin's role in Turkey's history in the wake of Rushdie's stabbing at the Chautauqua Institution, New York, in August 2022. In a recent speech, Freedom of Expression and its Champions, Sönmez drew parallels between enemies of free thought through the ages: "Rushdie and his book The Satanic Verses are not the first to be targeted. In the Middle Ages, Christian clergy like Calvin burned the clergy they had argued with, and Islamic rulers destroyed the books of Muslim thinkers like Avicenna," Sönmez said before speaking about the 1993 massacre.

"This act evokes the flames that ignited in the Middle Ages and was somehow forgotten by international platforms. Freedom of expression is not about banal platitudes but a concrete need that arises in the specifics of each work. This need is embodied today in Rushdie's name."

Today, one third of the Nesin Foundation's income comes from property Nesin had invested in while alive. Another third comes from donations. The final third comes from the royalties of Nesin's books, which sell around 250,000 and 280,000 copies annually. "Nesin is still among the most-read authors in Turkey," said Cihangiroğlu. "We sell more copies of his books than when he was alive."

Asked whether the ultimate aim of Rabıta was to drive him and the Nesin Foundation out of their home, Cihangiroğlu laughed. "If they want to wait for that, they'll wait a long time.

President of PEN International Burhan Sönmez on his idol Aziz Nesin:

Aziz Nesin and his generation shaped my life. In high school, I read most of his books. In our small town, we'd read books with my circle of friends and exchange volumes, as it wasn't easy to find books. I think his books were among those we read the most. Aziz Nesin was famed for his short stories and humorous tales, but I was most impressed by his book Surnâme. It's among his few novels, and its story is far from humorous. From that book, I learned that bad people, even those who commit crimes, could be good.

To find something good even in the most evil people, and to struggle to achieve good for humanity, must not have been easy for him. Aziz Nesin paid a heavy price for this through prison sentences, exile and censorship. In the last years of his life, he led the struggle for democracy against the 12 September 1980, military coup, and he defended freedom of expression against the ascendant fundamentalist movements.

When he and his followers published the Petition of Intellectuals, I was a university student studying law. A few months later, I had my own first experience of detention and torture. This wasn't an extraordinary occurrence at the time. Almost every family had a member who went through something similar. Those were times when the official cruelty of the Turkish state spread on all streets. During another detention, a decade later, I was taken to the Gayrettepe Police Headquarters in Istanbul for a torture session.

I was, by then, a young lawyer who followed human rights court cases. I was surprised to see how plainclothes police officers talked about Aziz Nesin instead of asking me questions. This was a few weeks before the Sivas Massacre. Their attitude showed that the Turkish state had amassed enough fury against Nesin. It was clear that the government had a spiritual affinity with Islamic groups: they were preparing something against Aziz Nesin. These were plainclothes police officers, and they have not tied my eyes in this instance, I think because I was a lawyer.

When I looked them in the eye and said that Aziz Nesin was an excellent writer and a good human being and that Turkey could become a much better place only if people listened to people like him, they were infuriated. Ignorance of freedom caused their violent attitude. They were trying to scare off people struggling for democracy and freedom.

I believe that from Aziz Nesin to Salman Rushdie, from Osman Kavala to Dawit Isaak, whoever struggles for this same aim today contributes to the shared culture of humanity. These artists and intellectuals base their work on principles and a commitment to values. They pursue the struggle for freedom, even when left in the minority.

I saw Aziz Nesin only once in my life. I was a student. I was in Cağaloğlu, preparing to buy a book from a distributor. The old elevator of the building must have been out of order. There was someone stuck in it. A doorman came and opened the door. And he said to the man trapped inside, "Okay, uncle, you can step out now."

The man who stepped out was Aziz Nesin. With the joy of seeing him, I stood in the corridor and watched him for a while. This was one of the happiest days of my life. I know that Turkey is like an elevator out of order. It's stuck. To rescue people trapped inside, we must open its faulty door.

Aziz Nesin is here, for one thing. His body is buried here. Even if we left, his body would haunt them forever." ✖

Kaya Genç is Index contributing editor (Turkey). He is based in Istanbul

52(03):69/72|DOI:10.1177/03064220231201310

Sharia law and disorder

Religious intolerance and mob violence are increasing in Nigeria, as **KOLA ALAPINNI** has witnessed while defending those charged with blasphemy

AN ACCUSATION IS made and rumours quickly circulate that someone has blasphemed.

Soon, a mob gathers and throws stones and sticks. Within minutes, it is mission accomplished.

This is just the latest extra-judicial killing in northern Nigeria – the gruesome murder of Usman Buda in Sokoto in June 2023.

Cases like this are on the rise. They come from within communities, spearheaded sometimes by those closest to the victims, fuelled by Islamic religious extremists with the tacit support of the government, which fails to bring the assailants to book. Those extremists might have been delighted by the delisting of Nigeria as a country of particular concern by the USA in 2021, after only being put on the list a year earlier due to violations of religious freedoms and violent attacks. The delisting was followed by a spike in killings.

During the Covid pandemic in 2020, two cases from the city of Kano caught everyone napping. In August, a Sharia court sentenced a minor, Omar Farouq Bashir, to 10 years' imprisonment for blasphemy. On the same day, the Islamic judge sentenced Yahaya Sharif-Aminu to death by hanging for the same charge. Neither had legal representation.

Bashir had just moved to Kano with his brother-in-law in search of greener pastures. While working as a dishwasher in a restaurant, his phone fell out of his pocket and another worker picked it up, refused to return it and taunted Bashir.

Bashir lost his temper and probably uttered a swear word. The other man, eager to teach the new boy from the village a lesson, reported him to Hisbah, the Islamic police, a few days later. They

ABOVE: Amina Ahmed, the wife of Mubarak Bala, at her home in Abuja, Nigeria on 11 March 2021; less than a year after her husband's arrest

whisked him away to detention and then he was sent to the Sharia court.

Sharif-Aminu's situation was more complicated. He is the son of an Islamic cleric and a gospel singer from the Tijaniyya Sufi Muslim order.

He was accused of praising his Tijaniyya Prophet above the Prophet Muhammad in a Whatsapp recording, which was quickly shared around various groups. A few days later, when Hisbah went to arrest Sharif-Aminu, a mob gathered in front of his family home

and pelted it with stones. They also looted the property, injuring his family.

Both Bashir and Sharif-Aminu were charged under a section of Sharia law which criminalises insulting a Prophet of God. The penalty is death by hanging.

The Islamic clerics in Kano State had issued a fatwa restraining any Muslim lawyers from coming to their defence, and both the state-sponsored Legal Aid Council and other lawyers refused to defend them in fear of reprisal attacks.

After the lockdown restrictions eased, the judge pronounced his sentences on both of them and they had 30 days to appeal. It was at this stage that I, under the interventionist vehicle the →

 Someone brought out petrol and another lit the match. Her body was set on fire

Yakubu's killers got off the hook and a
woman is in prison for raising awareness

→ Foundation for Religious Freedom, went in surreptitiously to file an appeal.

It was whilst filing Sharif-Aminu's appeal on 3 September 2020 that we found out about Bashir's travesty of justice as well. I returned to file our second appeal, this time for Bashir. The atmosphere was so politically charged that even the bailiffs were apprehensive about serving the court papers on the government for fear of being reprimanded. I had to use a courier.

Now we had two appeals to prepare for. One was to snatch Sharif-Aminu from the hangman's noose.

I gave the scoop to a dependable ally at Sahara Reporters before releasing it to the international press. Before I could bat an eyelid my phone was blowing up with calls for interviews from CNN, the BBC, Reuters and AFP. The UN Human Rights Office in Geneva also wanted to talk.

After a delay caused by the End SARS protests which rocked our nation, eventually the appeals were heard in November. In January 2021, the Appellate Division of the Kano State High Court quashed Bashir's conviction and set him free. The court agreed with us that he was a minor and he had no business in an adult court, especially without legal representation.

In both cases, we argued that the constitution prohibited the state government or the federal government from adopting the practice of Sharia law. We argued that Nigeria was a signatory to the African Charter on Human and Peoples' Rights and the International Covenant on Civil and Political Rights. We also drew the attention of the court to sections of the constitution which guaranteed religious freedom and freedom of expression.

Sharif-Aminu's was a more explosive case. The court overturned his death penalty but, curiously, sent his case to

the Sharia court again for a retrial. We appealed to the second highest court in Nigeria – the Court of Appeal.

On 12 May 2022, after a series of delays, the court was not able to sit due to an emergency.

We learnt that Deborah Samuel Yakubu had been lynched by a mob made up of her teacher-training college classmates in Sokoto. The pictures that came out on social media were horrific.

Yakubu, a Christian, had complained that a class Whatsapp group for coursework had been hijacked for the spread of Islamic verses. An argument ensued and she was alleged to have blasphemed. Yakubu was waylaid on her way to class and hit with sticks and stones by her classmates and others nearby. The security staff claimed to be overwhelmed by the mob and left her to her fate. Someone brought out petrol and another lit the match. Her body was set on fire.

Presidential candidate Atiku Abubakar tweeted in condemnation of Yakubu's murder – but the backlash from northern users of Twitter, who threatened not to vote for him, made him delete the tweet.

In Yakubu's case, 34 lawyers turned up to defend her suspected murderers. The police charged only two people from the mob that killed her, and not with murder but with public disturbance. Eventually, the matter was struck out of court due to a lack of diligent prosecution.

Rhoda Jatau, a mother of five, tried to draw attention to the murder by forwarding the video on Whatsapp. In May 2022, she was arrested for inciting the public – the same offence that those suspected of murdering Yakubu had been charged with. Yakubu's killers got off the hook and a woman is in prison for raising awareness.

Ethnic and religious violence is not new to Nigeria. The roots lie in the amalgamation of more than 250 ethnic tribes by the British colonial government, which produced two huge territories – essentially two artificial countries. The northern one was largely Muslim, agrarian, poor and less-educated than its more religiously diverse and tolerant southern neighbour. This singular action created a multi-religious, multi-ethnic, multi-lingual mixture. It was also the root of the heightened tension we have seen in recent times in Nigeria.

It was inconceivable to the colonial government to have extreme punishments under Islamic law such as stoning people to death for adultery, expressing a different religious opinion or converting from Islam. Thus, the British put an end to it. This was largely the case until the colonial government granted Nigeria independence in 1960.

It created an uneasy alliance of a north with remnants of Fulani jihadists, a Hausa population that struggled to come to terms with its own identity and a rebellious and proud Kanem-Bornu Empire; all shades of believers and non-believers in the middle-belt; and a southern Nigeria with all forms of religious belief or no belief at all – a Molotov cocktail waiting to be ignited. Therein lies the root of the uneasy alchemy known as Nigeria, and with it the futile search for religious tolerance and freedom.

If Sharia law in Nigeria was not new, what then could be responsible for the spike in religious intolerance we have witnessed in the last two decades? In 1999, democracy was restored in Nigeria after a harrowing military incursion. For the first time since Nigeria's independence (apart from brief spells in 1966 and 1976), Nigeria was not being led by a northerner. In retaliation, a governor in the northern Zamfara state, Ahmad Sani Yerima, returned the criminal aspects of Sharia law previously done away with by the

ABOVE: A group of women in Maiduguri, Borno State, Nigeria

colonial government. Eleven northern states followed in quick succession.

This was an affront to the constitution of the Federal Republic of Nigeria, which recognises Sharia law only to the extent of Islamic personal law, guiding things such as marriage, inheritance and succession.

Every few years, news filtered in from northern Nigeria about someone who had been accused of speaking against Islam or the Prophet. They were usually hacked or stoned to death or, if they were lucky, they were arrested and charged before the Sharia courts.

Usually, there would be an international outcry, NGOs would get involved and the charges would be dropped. Alternatively, the alleged offender would plead guilty and ask for mercy before being let off the hook for time served in detention.

Mubarak Bala perhaps knew this. The humanist was arrested for blasphemy and had been held for two years when he suddenly decided to plead guilty on the morning of his arraignment. He had not seen his baby son since his arrest, and he reasoned that if he pleaded guilty he would get off quickly. He was in for a shock. The judge sentenced him to 24 years' imprisonment, which his legal team has appealed.

As Bala and Jatau remain behind bars, so too does our client Sharif-Aminu. After we filed that first (successful) appeal for Bashir and learnt about Sharif-Aminu's case, we vowed not to leave either man behind. ✖

Kola Alapinni is an international human rights lawyer and the director of operations at the Foundation for Religious Freedom

52(03):73/75|DOI:10.1177/03064220231201311

Loose hair in Tehran

RIGHT: Women in Tehran defy
headscarf laws, March 2023

FARNAZ HAERI describes the current situation for hijab-less women in Iran's capital city, introducing an essay revisiting her first ventures with her head uncovered

FRIENDS AND RELATIVES living abroad who have visited Iran in the last few months can't get over scenes of women going hijab-less on the streets. They can hardly believe their eyes that there are so many of us – even if the numbers vary considerably from one neighbourhood to another. These visitors say things like: "No one outside Iran is going to believe this. Television news overseas doesn't do any of this justice. It's as if, overnight, Tehran had turned into Istanbul."

These well-meaning folk have a point, of course. In fact, I've always loved going to cities such as Istanbul for exactly the same reason. One sees the possibility of what Tehran could be, a city where the religious and the secular manage to live side-by-side. Even a friend of mine who never takes off her hijab in Tehran acknowledged the irony of feeling far more comfortable in Istanbul as a hijab-wearing woman than she does in Tehran. "For one thing, no one ever gives me evil looks in Istanbul for preferring my hijab," she said.

Once the flames of the protests began to calm in last winter, it was still a novelty to see women in public without some sort of head covering. Folk would either applaud the few courageous trailblazers or curse at them. Half a year later, being without a hijab is nothing if not ordinary,

a part of the landscape of our cities. Still, the "men of the regime" (and I use the Persian term *dowlat-mard* quite deliberately) are hellbent on reimposing their will any way they can. Not a day passes without rumours and speeches about exorbitant fines to be imposed on women, or those not wearing hijabs being barred from jobs or denied social welfare or, even worse, being handed jail terms. This is all scary. And, yes, we women are scared. Who wouldn't be?

In parliament, swathes of hours each week are spent giving speeches not on the country's dire economic situation or Iran's diplomatic relations with other countries but on the hijab issue. Even though the morality police have been taken off the streets, recent reports suggest they will return under a different name. This pattern of simply changing a dreaded official entity's designation in the Islamic Republic is hardly new; it's been done before. There is talk about the authorities hiring "hijab patrols". So far, there's no sign of them, but the penalties and summonses are real. Actresses who have publicly taken off their hijabs are being called in for questioning and banned from work, and photos of cars with hijab-less women in them bring stiff fines to the vehicle owners' doors. In the meantime, any number of businesses and sports clubs are being shut down until further notice because women have been spotted there without head coverings.

The narrative on the hijab – its various iterations and its trajectory ever since the revolution – has been one of the more interesting aspects of the Islamic Republic. In the early days, if instead of a traditional *chador* (a full-body and hair cloak) you wore the equivalent of a

long robe or overcoat (a *manteau*), the regime simply would not give you the time of day – not for government jobs nor for admission to higher education. Nevertheless, in time the *manteau* itself became shorter and shorter while women wore more and more makeup and flaunted it. When a *manteau* went from being ankle-length to being knee-length for the first time, those of us who made the leap were ecstatic. Today, the knee-length *manteau* is so mainstream that even anchors on official state television wear them in front of the camera. Furthermore, no one considers the knee-length *manteau* "short" anymore. The truth is that the hijab, by default, became something of a fashion statement. Those women who did not like it or want it learned to own it anyway, until this past year when those same women chose to throw away their hijabs altogether.

There is a catch, though: unlike family and friends visiting from abroad, I'm not jumping for joy over any of this. To see women without hijabs or women freely riding bicycles and even motorcycles leaves me mostly cold and sad. Because my reality is not the reality of our guests from abroad or our Western sympathisers and counterparts. Our reality is the poverty we see on the streets every day, the international economic sanctions that strangle us and the everyday fear from the regime concocting new laws. Besides, how are we to live with the memory of all those we lost this past year, through pitched street battles, incarcerations and executions? Where is the joy to follow from that? The only thing we can do is to pretend life goes on and everything is normal. Pretend that there is hope still, and that somehow there will be light at the end of this decades-long struggle.

Farnaz Haeri is a translator, researcher and essayist based in Tehran

Translated from Persian by Salar Abdoh

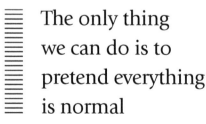

The only thing we can do is to pretend everything is normal

Braving Tehran's Roundabout, Maidan Valiasr

By Farnaz Haeri

MY HEAD IS uncovered, so is my neck. As soon as I meet the eyes of the policeman standing near the bus stop, my hands automatically reach for my hijab. Then I remember that, of course, I'm not wearing one. A minute later, when I get on the bus, people who still aren't used to seeing women without a headscarf glance at me and quickly turn away, their eyes full of questions. At the next station, an austere-looking woman wrapped in her black *chador*, prayer beads in hand, gets on. She fingers her prayer beads and repeats an invocation under her breath. There's bound to be a fight between us, I think to myself. Instead, what does she do? She asks me for directions, and

I tell her she needs to get off at the next stop. Her gratitude is a wave of kindness: 'May you always be safe, my daughter. Please take very good care of yourself.'

I hadn't expected this. Nor did I expect it yesterday at the photocopy shop when the man stood up, bowed in my direction, and said, 'Long live our courageous women!' Nowadays, instead of being pestered on the streets by young men, women are met with the refrain of the movement: Woman, Life, Freedom. This too is as unexpected as it is beautiful.

I get off the bus at Maidan Valiasr, in the heart of the city. I have to pass through the →

My heart is in my mouth. I expect a baton to collide with my head at any moment

This hair is not going to lead any young man astray with desire

→ eastern end of the circle, which is where the undercovers and Basij militia are assembled. So far, the entire city has paid my curls nothing but respect. But not these guys. As I pass by them, one of them says to the man next to him, 'I bet if I hit her over the head she'd pass out.' He laughs as he says this, loud enough that I can hear it. My heart is in my mouth, I expect a baton to collide with my head at any moment. As I continue walking, looking directly ahead, someone hits me in the ribs – maybe with the butt of a gun – and shouts at me to cover my head. I don't have anything to cover my head with, and I wouldn't do it even if I did. My hands stay by my side and I press on ahead. Another one of them shouts, 'Dirty Bahai, cover that head.' The next man adds, 'Bahai slut'. I hadn't realised until now that, to these men, calling someone a 'Bahai' – a member of a much-abused religious minority that got its start in Iran in the nineteenth century – is the ultimate insult. In the meantime, I'm still waiting for that baton to hit my head as I finally march past the end of the line-up of street thugs.

The maidan at Valiasr has for many years had a gigantic billboard space on its northwest quadrant. I still don't dare look up, expecting that at any moment something, anything, is going to knock me flat to the ground. When I finally muster enough courage to look, I notice that, on the several-stories-high billboard, there's nothing but a vast blank space and below it the words: 'The Women of My Land.' The absurdity of seeing these words in reference to nothing and no one is as strange as hearing paid street thugs call you a Bahai slut. The billboard looks orphaned with just those words serving as signifiers to something nonexistent. When it was first put up, the faces of real Iranian women, heads of course properly covered, had been up there – supposedly the

regime's way of fighting back against the Woman, Life, Freedom refrain of the street demonstrations. But there was such an outcry by the people featured and their relatives that the regime was forced to remove their photos, leaving only a string of forlorn words on a massive vacant poster.

I keep on walking. Walking without that dreaded piece of cloth they've forced on us since the first year in school. The piece of cloth that clawed at my throat throughout my younger years would often slip off without me realising it. That piece of cloth is gone. Gone from my head and from those of many others. For us it's as if the Berlin Wall has finally come down.

I've run a gauntlet and a fire of insults and I'm still in one piece. The fear is still with me, but it's only lurking in the background. Our world here has shifted. Those militia goons can say what they want; the truth is that not wearing a hijab no longer means being a loose woman or a 'slut' in this country. It no longer creates a feeling of us-versus-them. We Iranians are all in this together. And no one is going to hang us from our hair in hell anymore. In primary school, the religious studies teacher insisted this is what would befall us if we were seen outside in public without our hijabs. The image of being strung up by my hair in hell was so traumatic that I begged my parents to take me to the barber and cut off all my hair like a boy's. I figured no one would be able to hang me from my hair if I didn't have any in the first place.

Nowadays, loose hair – without a forced casing of fabric around it – is simply hair. Nothing more, nothing less. This hair is not going to lead any young man astray with desire. At the very least, the people on the streets of my city have realised this. Maybe one day the country's religious studies teachers will get it too. ✖

*Translated from Persian by **Salar Abdoh***

Published from the upcoming book Woman Life Freedom: Voices and Art from the Women's Protests in Iran, edited by Malu Halasa and published by Saqi Books in September 2023

52(03):76/78|DOI:10.1177/03064220231201312

Handmaid's Tale in Holy Land

As women's faces are scrubbed from public life upon orders from Israel's increasingly political orthodox wing, **JO-ANN MORT** speaks to some of those fighting back

DEMANDS BY ULTRA-ORTHODOX rabbis to exempt women's voices from state-sponsored public performances and their faces from public advertisements were growing in Israel even before a right-wing, religious-fundamentalist government was elected in 2023. Now, with a government heavily dependent on ultra-orthodox parties (which ban women's representation in their parliamentary lists), the threat has increased.

Two of the women leading the fight against this are lawyer and director of the Israel Religious Action Centre (IRAC) Orly Erez-Likhovski and Moran Zer Katzenstein, the founder and director of a new group, Bonot Alternativa. In the midst of massive summer protests against the government, they each took time to talk about the situation.

"The government has a lot of initiatives and bills trying to curtail women's rights," Erez-Likhovski told me. IRAC is affiliated with the Movement for Reform and Progressive Judaism in Israel, part of the worldwide reform/liberal Jewish movement. In contrast to orthodoxy, reform and liberal movements take a more "modern" approach. Synagogues, for example, typically have mixed seating rather than separate seating for men and women.

"They want to expand gender segregation" in the public sphere, Erez-Likhovski said of the current government. One bill that has been introduced demands that the Israel Nature and Parks Authority establishes separate bathing times for men and women for at least 15% of the operating hours while increasing the number of gender-segregated beaches.

"They are considering a bill to allow

ABOVE: Anti-government protesters dressed like the handmaids from The Handmaid's Tale demonstrate against the government's state budget in front of the Knesset, 23 May 2023, Jerusalem

people to refuse services based on their religious beliefs. For instance, a public bus driver could deny entry to a woman if she is not dressed modestly. Also, they want to completely politicise the Authority for the Advancement of Women."

Once a professional body, this office is now run by a government minister (a woman who is vehemently anti-foreign worker and anti-feminist).

At the end of July, Benjamin Netanyahu's government passed legislation to neuter the Supreme Court. A photo of government ministers applauding their victory included two female ministers, but their faces were obscured in the ultra-orthodox media. The same media blocked out Hillary Clinton's photo when she was US secretary of state.

Ultra-orthodox pressure has blocked out women in supermarket advertisements, on billboards, in doctors' offices and elsewhere for some time now. The famed Jerusalem Film Festival gave up promotion with street posters that included women years ago, due to ultra-orthodox pressure. This past summer's posters featured two horse heads that somehow were meant to symbolise cutting-edge cinema.

"It's a spectrum that starts with not allowing any woman to be seen in the public sphere and then trying to →

 The Israeli public has a lot of power – businesses respond to this power and outrage

CREDIT: Eddie Gerald / Alamy

→ actually eliminate women physically," Erez-Likhovski said.

"We have fought the Jerusalem municipality for many years against the tsunami of not allowing images of women to be shown on billboards. Although the court said they have to work together with the police against this, they're doing nothing."

Yet, even under the rule of the right-wing government – and maybe also because of it – Erez-Likhovski observed that "responsiveness of the Israeli public to women's rights in general and exclusion of women in particular has dramatically changed". She added: "Years ago, people were mostly indifferent to these practices. Today, it really enrages people and reaches major headlines."

She gave the example of a pharmacy in the ultra-orthodox neighbourhood of Bnei Brak that recently covered up the images of women on hair products. Within two days, its policy had been changed.

"The Israeli public has a lot of power – businesses respond to this power and outrage. I think it's important, especially with this kind of government," she said.

Previous decisions that once protected women will doubtless be revisited now that the government has passed a law limiting the Supreme Court's power to rule against government decisions. The controversial new law cancelled what is known as the "reasonableness clause", which is similar to British common law. Many issues related to religion and state and minority rights, the rights of women and more were decided this way. Unless the law is overturned on

You need to get involved because they are changing the rules of the game

appeal, it will stick – at least until there is a different government.

One reason for the introduction of this law is the quest for power by the ultra-orthodox. In Israel, the ultra-orthodox rabbinate makes decisions over rituals for all Jewish citizens. Moderate streams of Judaism hold significantly less legal power. IRAC has won significant victories against the ultra-orthodox stranglehold in court but now it will be nearly impossible to do so, because of the manipulation of the courts by this government.

There is no legal civil marriage, though common law marriage is recognised – for now. Instead all marriages in Israel are religious ones and

that means only a rabbinic court can provide a legal divorce. Needless to say, it's uncommon for these rabbis to decide in favour of the woman. The rabbinate can even rule whether or not a woman can lead a prayer mourning a relative at a funeral, since almost all funerals are run by state-supported ultra-orthodox rabbis. Now the government wants to expand issues that these courts handle, including alimony – a fraught issue that can lead to family violence.

And violence against women is of growing concern in Israel. The previous government began to tighten laws against spousal abuse, but now the orthodox nationalist minister in charge of homeland security thinks that this

LEFT: A partition separating men and women in prayer at the Western Wall

me, 'Moran, you need to get involved because they are changing the rules of the game'. We were seven women with red shirts. The week afterwards, we were 15 women. The week after, we were 50 and growing exponentially.

Zer Katzenstein said one of the activists suggested they mimic The Handmaid's Tale, three of them stayed up all night to sew the caps and then a team of 20 walked from the Supreme Court to the Knesset in Jerusalem.

"People were in shock. We were silent, walking in pairs, looking at the floor. By the time we got to the Knesset, everyone photographed it."

Since then dramatic displays of columns of handmaidens have appeared at large protest rallies in Israel, and even in expat Israeli democracy rallies in London and New York.

"We have an activist who is a professor of gender studies who said, 'We are reclaiming the word handmaid because now, in Israel, when you say handmaid, you know this is the red women – they're fighters'."

In July, Supreme Court president Esther Hayut, who is set to retire in October, announced she will convene the entire 15-member court in September to hear appeals over the abolition of the "reasonableness" law. Usually Supreme Court appeals are heard by a small panel of judges, but these are not usual times. The hearing could lead to a constitutional crisis, since Netanyahu has not agreed to abide by the court if it rules against his government.

By now, there's little doubt that Israel's women will be in the streets cheering on the court as they seek to protect their rights. ✖

Jo-Ann Mort is a journalist based in Israel and the USA

legislation is "unfair" to men.

"This government refused to join the Istanbul Convention, which says that countries should protect women, women's security and safety," Erez-Likhovski noted. No surprise there.

Meanwhile, Zer Katzenstein's new feminist organisation is ensuring that Israeli women promote the threats of their disappearance in a clever and dramatic manner.

They burst into the public imagination partly due to their costumes, in the red gowns and white bonnets of the handmaidens created by Margaret Atwood in The Handmaid's Tale and popularised by the show.

Zer Katzenstein created Bonot

Alternativa simply by starting a WhatsApp group and inviting women to a conversation. She was so incensed by a gang rape three years ago in Israel that she felt she had to do something.

"We held 30 midday strikes around the country and one big one in Rabin Square [in front of Tel Aviv's City Hall]. The biggest companies in Israel joined. I built a grassroots organisation, so anyone with an idea or initiative could contribute," she said.

The group includes women from all sectors – right wing, left wing, religious, social, orthodox and Arab women.

She said: "[After the elections,] I sat in the kitchen with my husband looking at the television and he told

52(03):79/81|DOI:10.1177/03064220231201316

Practise what they preach

The UAE talks about how it values tolerance while actively discriminating against the country's LGBTQ+ community. **SIMON COATES** talks to those affected

NTOLERANCE DISGUISED AS benevolence is a pillar of Emirati society, with the country's values often cited as a justification for prejudice. Such was the case last September 2022, when the UAE government's Ministry of Education announced a new code of conduct that included a clause forbidding education professionals from "discussing gender identity, homosexuality or any other behavior deemed unacceptable to the UAE's

society" in the country's educational establishments. In a tweet, the UAE's Education Minister, Dr Ahmad Belhoul Al Falasi, said, "we are proud of our educational professions and we are keen to consolidate the values of the UAE society according to the directives of the wise leadership."

Same-sex relationships and transgender individuals are criminalised in the country, and the new code of conduct is the latest in a history of

ABOVE: People preparing for iftar in front of a mosque in the modern Business Bay district of Dubai, April 2023

legislation that uses the values trope as a mode of subjugation. "Censorship is part of everyday life in the UAE," said Radha Stirling, CEO of Detained in Dubai, the organisation that ensures the security of foreign nationals in the Gulf. "Given the country's Muslim roots, it's unsurprising that authorities have explicitly prohibited

CREDIT: Viktor Pazemin/Alamy

classroom education in relation to gender and homosexuality."

Chapter 2, verse 256 of the Koran is often cited as a call for tolerance - its maxim "there should be no compulsion in religion" - suggests no one should force opinions on others. The customs and values central to Emirati social legislation - tolerance included - are largely legitimated by Islam doctrine and, in 2016, the UAE government founded its own Ministry of Tolerance and Coexistence to "promote an environment of human fraternity and peaceful coexistence". One of the Ministry's first moves was to partner with the Hay Festival for the first UAE iteration in Abu Dhabi. Yet, despite the Ministry's aim of using the partnership to illustrate their commitment to tolerance and understanding, one of the British festival organisers accused the UAE's Tolerance Minister, Sheikh Nahyan bin Mubarak Al Nahyan, of sexual assault during a meeting about the event in his private villa in 2020. Al Nahyan refuted the accusation.

Last year the UAE welcomed the Pope to the country, the regime using the exercise as another illustration of its move towards a more tolerant society. However, in the same year, the UAE government requested Netflix remove "offensive content" in an apparent targeting of programmes featuring LGBTQ+ characters that "contradict Islamic and societal values and principles". Amazon removed access to LGBTQ+ products - books, Pride flags - from their regional site at the request of the Emirati authorities. Transgender model Rachaya Noppakaroon told her Facebook followers how she'd been denied entry into the UAE as her passport showed her gender as male. In their 2022 report, Out Leadership, the organisation that supports LGBTQ+ business leaders worldwide, warned that "the UAE is one of a few countries in the world that prohibit transgender women's very existence, punishing 'any male dressed in female apparel' with a prison term".

While Koranic teachings can be seen to preach tolerance, they are also used to justify the positions of those expressing anti-LGBTQ+ sentiments in the UAE. Last September, US-based international law firm Baker McKenzie severed ties with their senior partner in the Emirates, Habib Al Mulla, after he posted tweets to his 61,000 followers using religious standpoints to denounce homosexuality as "evil" and a "perversion". Al Mulla also used Twitter to comment on a social media video celebrating Emirati Women's Day. The film showed one Emirati woman saying, "No matter what you look like or feel inside you are not alone". Al Mulla saw this as a thinly disguised promotion of homosexuality, tweeting that "there is a children's story for gay marketing entitled 'How You Feel Inside'" and "as for the phrase 'You are not alone', it is used frequently in gay publications", before going on to equate homosexuality with "paedophilia and atheism". After the news of the split broke, Twitter users defended Al Mulla's stance. One account posted Koranic text referencing the city of Sodom that was punished by Allah for celebrating same-sex relationships before going on to declare, "homosexuality is a setback for human instinct, and a dangerous deviation from the laws of God almighty".

"In the West, pioneering liberal views are a challenge for Western societies. For the UAE, they are totally foreign concepts," British academic Matthew Hedges told Index. Hedges was carrying out research in the UAE in May 2018 when he was arrested on spying charges and sentenced to life in prison in the country. He was pardoned later the same year. For Hedges, the UAE's recent ramping up of anti-LGBTQ+ censorship is linked to a domestic conflict of interests. While the UAE longs to be seen as modern and progressive, its heteronormative communal values remain pegged to religious ideology.

"The idea of discussing gender norms and homosexuality is a highly

Social conservatism has risen as a reaction to modernisation

contentious issue for the native national community," he said.

"Should this community become altered by foreign gender norm re-evaluations or a liberal view of homosexuality, it will fragment their traditional view of the family. Think of it as Republican US, but with a related national community." Hedges also sees a link between social conservatism and religious extremism in the UAE. "Social conservatism has risen as a reaction to modernisation, globalisation and hyper development," he said. "The state is trying to balance this."

Born in Abu Dhabi and now living in the USA, a person who wanted to be referred to simply as Noon is a transfeminine Emirati. Speaking of their time in the UAE, they said, "as I grew older I recognised more aspects of censorship by things deemed inappropriate in Islam. As an openly queer 15-year old Emirati, it was easy to censor me by making me not exist. I was told 'Arabs can't be queer' and 'you're just mentally ill'."

Unmoved by the UAE's new legislation, Noon manages to find a glimpse of positivity in its theme. "It means that more young people are talking about their queerness, which I didn't have any access to as a youth," they said. "The fact is, these laws won't stop us from being queer. They give me hope that some man with power is scared of us because we're not so silent and hidden anymore." ✖

Simon Coates is a London-based writer, who lived in the UAE between 2011 and 2017

52(03):82/83|DOI:10.1177/03064220231201317

CREDIT: SOPA Images Limited / Alamy

Poland's papal problem

With elections around the corner in Poland, a row over the reputation of a former Pope is being used for political gain – but that's not the only worrying way religion is exploited in the country, writes **KSENIYA TARASEVICH**

" I DIDN'T CONSIDER THE
repercussions when I took that action,"
Zofia Nierodzińska, an artist, curator
and writer, told Index.

In the midst of extensive protests in

Poland against the introduction of anti-
abortion laws in 2020, Nierodzińska
hurled three eggs at the Church of the
Elevation of the Holy Cross in Poznań.

As a result, she faced legal charges for

disrespecting a public space designated
for religious ceremonies.

"I don't consider my act as something
emotional. It was the least I could do
while watching the Catholic Church take

LEFT: Polish men, who gather every first Saturday of the month to pray and beg forgiveness for blasphemy during the monthly Men's Rosary at the Main Square, in Krakow on 4 January 2020

Polish women's rights away," she said. "Its work causes deaths. It was just my reaction to the crimes that are happening in Poland."

Nierodzińska no longer lives in Poland. She says that her decision to move away was influenced by, among other things, this "fascism and feudalism that thrives in Poland, and the threats I was receiving" – including, she said, being spied on by police.

The Polish constitution states a division between the Catholic Church and the state, but the reality is very different. Under the current ruling right-wing Law and Justice party (PiS), religious groups have further infiltrated politics.

Dominika Bychawska-Siniarska, a human rights expert, told Index: "The authorities favour the Church. And they exploit the power. Polish authorities flirt with the Church. Many politicians share these values, therefore allowing it to have a stronger voice. The Church gains additional privileges."

The Catholic Church has always played a central role in Poland – and at times for the better. During the communist era, for example, it emerged as a prominent symbol of resistance. Despite the prohibition on religion in most Warsaw Pact nations, including Poland, the Catholic Church garnered substantial backing and influence. The assassination of Solidarity-supporting priest Jerzy Popiełuszko in 1984 further intensified the strained relationship between the Church and the communist regime. Attending church services symbolised an act of defiance.

However, underlying tensions persisted, and beneath the surface the conservative nationalism held by numerous priests clashed strongly with the secular liberalism embraced by many prominent dissidents. Although the Church was anti-communism, it was not necessarily supportive of free speech, individualism and liberalisation. After 1989, when the Church was legalised for the first time under communist rule, it resumed its central role in the public sphere. It regained land and property it had lost after World War II, and clergymen attended secular celebrations, including the opening of McDonald's restaurants. Few parties ever openly opposed or contradicted it. Even Aleksander Kwaśniewski, the former president of Poland who was on the far left, met the Pope on several occasions.

But it is in the PiS that the Catholic Church has really been centred. Under the PiS – members of which are open about their faith – the Church has received a record amount of money from the public budget and their views have become more influential.

The Archbishop of Kraków called the LGBTQ+ community a "rainbow plague" and, rather than such sentiment being dismissed or ignored, it's became a template for others. From 2019, hundreds of regions across Poland — about a third of the country, with more than 10 million citizens — transformed themselves into "LGBT-free zones" in an effort to fit more in with "family" and "historic Christian" values. And the Church's hardline conservative stance on women's rights influenced the near-total ban on abortions imposed by the Constitutional Tribunal of Poland.

Perhaps no one symbolises how the Church still dominates, and how religion is exploited, in Poland today better than Pope John Paul II, who was sovereign of the Vatican City State from 1978 until his death in 2005. Born Karol Wojtyla in Poland, he is credited with helping end communism in the country and is widely revered. But this year his reputation was dealt a blow when a documentary aired on US-owned broadcaster TVN alleged that when he was a cardinal in Kraków, his home city, he protected priests accused of sexually molesting children. →

It was the least I could do while watching the Catholic Church take Polish women's rights away

→   In response to the claims –
which some have said are based on
unreliable sources – PiS struck back.
US ambassador Mark Brzezinski
was summoned (later toned down to
"invited") to the foreign ministry. PiS
then pushed through a parliamentary
resolution "in defence of the good
name of Pope John Paul II" which read:
"The [parliament] strongly condemns
the shameful campaign conducted by
the media … against the Great Pope
St John Paul II, the greatest Pole in
history." The government and its
affiliated media launched a campaign
in his name. Public broadcaster TVP
aired a daily papal sermon, while a
large picture of the Pope was projected
on the façade of the presidential palace
in Warsaw.

As religion and politics intertwine
and people's bodies become a
battleground, speech is also being
regulated and blasphemy charges have
increased. Data shows a correlation
between the occurrences of "offences
against religious rights" cases and the
ruling party in Poland. The lowest
count was observed in 2011 when the
pro-EU party Platforma Obywatelska
(Civic Platform) was in office. In 2020,
this number surged to 97 cases under
the conservative PiS administration.
In March this year, a court found two
women guilty of offending religious
feelings simply for displaying an image of
the Virgin Mary and Jesus with rainbow
haloes during an LGBTQ+ march.
One was ordered to do five months of
community service while the other was
fined 2,000 zloty (about $500).

Originally, Article 196 of the Polish
Criminal Code was designed to protect

The authorities favour the Church. And they exploit the power

religious minorities (including Jews
who were, for centuries, the victims
of pogroms in Poland and then the
Holocaust).

Now it's the opposite. It takes just
one accusation – even an anonymous
one – saying "my religious feelings are
offended" to start prosecution. Last year,
a junior partner in the ruling coalition
proposed toughening the blasphemy law
to allow anyone who "publicly insults
the Church" or interrupts mass to be
jailed for up to three years. The ruling
party did not support that bill, but
later justice minister Zbigniew Ziobro
submitted a proposal to parliament,
signed by more than 400,000 people,
calling for the law to be broadened by
abolishing the requirement of proof that
somebody has been offended, among
other things.

The most common punishments are
fines and community service. Although
the maximum punishment can be up to
two years in prison, this is very rare and
usually reserved for repeat offenders or if
paired with another offence.

Even though it is an EU member state,
there is not much the EU can do about
the rule of law in Poland. As in Hungary,
which is also led by a right-wing party
with links to the Church, the EU has
proven largely ineffective at intervening.

"Considering our government's
existing stance on adhering to the
directives of the European Court of
Human Rights, which they are obligated
to enact and follow through on, it
seems that they are indifferent," said
Bychawska-Siniarska. "Taking a rational
approach, it would be wise to consider
abolishing the imprisonment penalty for
actions that are seen as disrespectful to
religious sentiments."

That said, in a rare victory, the
ECtHR recently ruled that a charge of
blasphemy in Poland from 10 years ago
against the singer Dorota Rabczewska
(known as Doda) violated her human
rights. Polish authorities have been
ordered to pay €10,000 in damages.

Perhaps surprisingly, Poland has one

of the highest secularisation rates in the
world, Konrad Talmont-Kamiński, a
professor at the University of Białystok,
told Index. When church attendance,
personal prayer, declared religiosity,
religious affiliation and supernatural
beliefs are considered, there is a huge
generational divide in the country. He
said: "A very typical thing in Poland
is to see a person who claims to be
a Catholic. But when you ask them,
'When did you last go to church?'
the answer could be, 'A long while
ago, when my nephew had his first
communion a year ago.' Religion plays
no role in this person's life."

But religion is important for the
PiS. The Church continues to have
disproportionate influence among the
elderly and those living in smaller towns
and villages, all of which are PiS's
electoral strongholds. Defending its
honour is a way to shore up support and
attack any opposition. This is crucial
ahead of the upcoming general elections,
set to take place on 15 October.

Young voters are expected to turn out
in large numbers, amid calls by the far-
right for an even harder line on women's
and LGBTQ+ rights. Will the PiS lose
power, and in so doing allow Poles some
distance from the Church and to regain
some liberties lost?

Bychawska-Siniarska believes that the
status quo in Poland is hard to change.

"The interaction between the Polish
state and the Church relies heavily on
a significant level of agreement," she
said. "Therefore, even if a leader with
more progressive viewpoints assumes
power, altering this process will remain
highly challenging."

If Poland's history tells us
anything, Bychawska-Siniarska is
right – which is a disaster for anyone
who wishes to live their life free from
religious interference. ✖

*Kseniya Tarasevich is a freelance journalist
from Poland. She is based in Poznań*

52(03):84/86|DOI:10.1177/03064220231201318

COMMENT

"This MI5 officer is almost certainly dead unless
he is more than 100 years old, so it is hard to
understand the rationale behind such censorship"

MARK HOLLINGSWORTH | TRUTH IN SEDUCTION | P.90

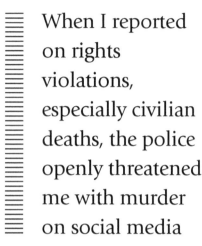

When I reported on rights violations, especially civilian deaths, the police openly threatened me with murder on social media

journalism in Kurdish cities. After the Turkish-Kurdish peace process failed, intense clashes broke out. Basic human rights, including the right to life, were being violated during the conflict. Journalists who publicised these violations were targeted.

I was one of them.

For me, the first link in the chain of cruelty was this story.

On 5 August 2015, masked Turkish police officers raided a construction site in Yüksekova, my hometown on the border between Iraq and Iran. The police tortured Kurdish workers who were forced to lie face down, handcuffed behind their backs, half-naked on the ground. The police shouted at the workers: "What the hell did this state do to you? You will see the power of the Turks!"

After I publicised the footage of the raid and the torture, I was systematically targeted. I was subjected to police surveillance, harassment and threats. They did not bother to respond to the criminal complaints I filed through my lawyers.

When I reported on rights violations, especially civilian deaths, the police openly threatened me with murder on social media. On 12 May 2016, I was detained by masked police officers. They forced me to the ground, like the workers, and beat me. They even stamped on my back. Upon my

Turkish and European courts failed me

Recently released political prisoner **NEDIM TÜRFENT** discusses his own case and why he feels let down by the European Court of Human Rights

AS TURKEY TURNED into a prison for freedom of thought and journalism or, as the government claims, is it the case that "they are not journalists, they are terrorists"? I am one of those who has been labelled a "terrorist". I could laugh about the label, but the label has taken

six-and-a-half years from me, which is not funny at all. I want to tell you my story and you can decide for yourself whether I fit the label. Surely this is the fairest way to decide.

I started my journalism career in 2012, at the Dicle News Agency, and for years I reported on rights-based

detention, my lawyers, my family and journalist organisations called the prosecutor's office, but state authorities refused to acknowledge my detention for hours. A campaign was launched: Where is Nedim Türfent?

After torturing me, the police put me in a car and took me to a hill. They put a black bag over my head, tied my hands behind my back and debated whether to kill me. Finally, one of them made a phone call and it was decided they wouldn't kill me. Hours later they admitted that I had been detained and informed my lawyers.

On 13 May I was formally arrested. That same summer there was an attempted coup in Turkey and a state of emergency was declared. For 13 months I waited for my indictment to be prepared until the trial finally began. The prosecution had 20 witnesses, but they all refuted the charges against me. Instead, they told the judges one by one that the police had forced them to testify against me. One of them opened his mouth and showed it to the judge, saying: "The police pulled out this tooth with pliers to make me testify against Nedim. I was tortured."

All the witnesses rejected the statements they gave under torture, and the police plot was exposed.

Despite requests from my lawyers and me I was not allowed to physically attend the hearings – which is illegal. I had to make my defence from prison via video conference, and my defence in my native Kurdish was not properly translated into Turkish.

My journalism was then declared a "crime". The court sentenced me to eight years and nine months in prison without the slightest concrete evidence. In the verdict, the court admitted the reason for the sentence: "Nedim Türfent was punished for making disturbing news..."

....

OPPOSITE: Türfent in London after serving a seven-year prison sentence; RIGHT: Türfent in prison, where his treatment improved once his case was on the international radar

We appealed the decision, but our objections were rejected. While we appealed, two important developments took place that should have had a direct impact on my case. First, the Constitutional Court, the highest court in Turkey, ruled in a decision that "expressions for news purposes do not constitute a crime even if they are shocking and disturbing."

Secondly, in the judicial reform package enacted in 2019, the same phrase was added to the relevant article of the Anti-Terror Law. Still, our appeal was rejected. As a last resort, we took the case to the European Court of Human Rights.

I was released on 29 November 2022, after six years and seven months. But the ECtHR has still not taken on my case.

I was arrested at the age of 26 and released when I was 33. How will I be compensated and how will the cruelty be penalised? On top of how Turkish courts acted, my belief in justice is disappearing day-by-day. With rights violations so blatant, the ECtHR needs to either conclude cases faster or find a new formula. It is a human rights court and it is obliged to do what is necessary to protect our human rights.

During my dark period, many organisations such as Index on Censorship campaigned for me. Certainly, their support and solidarity

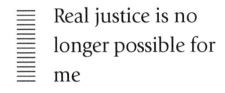

Real justice is no longer possible for me

eased my prison conditions. I took comfort in knowing I had not been forgotten and the guards treated me better too. All of this I am incredibly grateful for.

But should the only duty of NGOs, especially freedom of expression organisations, be to show support and solidarity?

In my story there was a grotesque injustice. None of us can fight such a thing alone. In my humble opinion the NGOs who have a stake in rights and freedom need a process of discussion and brainstorming to encourage the ECtHR to rule quickly. How can we stand up against such blatant injustices? How can we object? We should be asking these questions moving forward.

I have experienced injustice to the fullest. Real justice is no longer possible for me. But it's not too late for others in similar situations. ✖

Nedim Türfent is a journalist and editor of the press agency Bianet

....

52(03):88/89|DOI:10.1177/03064220231201319

Truth in seduction

We could learn a lot from a historical honey trap. But Whitehall's culture of secrecy stops us, writes **MARK HOLLINGSWORTH**

NVESTIGATING AND WRITING about the secret state is not easy. Secrecy and censorship governing access to intelligence archives are endemic and institutionalised. I discovered this daunting reality during my research for my book on KGB covert operations in the West during the Cold War. Late one night I read a reference to the KGB honey-trapping and destroying the career of the UK Conservative MP Anthony Courtney in 1965.

A vociferous critic of the Soviet Union and the KGB throughout the Cold War, the former Royal Navy intelligence officer spoke Russian and travelled to Moscow as a consultant to UK firms selling their products to eastern Europe. He loved Russia, but the problem was he loved Russian women more. And so he was a prime target for the KGB.

In 1961, a vivacious "tourist guide" was tasked by the KGB to seduce the gullible MP in a Moscow hotel room. Their brief encounter was covertly recorded with hidden cameras and stored in the files. At this stage the KGB would usually blackmail the target. But this time they waited.

Meanwhile, in the House of Commons, Courtney continued to attack the Soviet Union and claimed the KGB conducted nefarious criminal operations in the UK using the cover of diplomatic immunity. He argued all the staff in the Soviet embassy in London enjoyed immunity, even though 60% of them were KGB officers.

This criticism produced a sharp reaction from the KGB. It was time to strike.

In August 1965, an anonymous package containing the incriminating photographs was sent to 10 Downing Street, the House of Commons, Courtney's Conservative Association and his Labour party opponent. Attached to the pictures was a note accusing the married MP of shady activities. It was a crude attempt to inflict maximum political damage. The message was clear: stop criticising the Soviet Union – or else.

Clearly there were security implications, and Courtney met the prime minister, Harold Wilson, and his intelligence adviser, George Wigg, who had also received the photographs and an attached note which concluded: "To be continued…"

MI5 was told to investigate, and it established the dossier originated from the Soviet Union (later leaked documents proved it was the KGB using the codename Operation PROBA).

Courtney's Conservative Association at Harrow East regarded the scandal as "political dynamite". He was now under huge pressure. He barely survived a deselection vote, and at the next year's general election lost his previously safe seat by 378 votes after two recounts. Courtney left the political arena and retired.

The KGB had removed its most trenchant critic from parliament and the episode illustrated the insidious

power of the Russian security services, which today still remain very active throughout the West – especially in Ukraine – using disinformation, hacking and assassination.

But how could I chronicle the case with primary documents? For the historian it was the ultimate challenge. Do you accept the official version of events, or do you dig deeper? I chose the latter on the basis that nearly all memoirs of politicians, diplomats and intelligence officers omit and conceal salient facts.

The mysterious Wigg, the prime minister's intelligence troubleshooter, was a case in point. There was not one reference to the Courtney affair in his autobiography and no documents at the National Archives or in the MP's papers at the Imperial War Museum.

And so I took a chance. I visited Wigg's personal archive at the London School of Economics, and buried in the dusty old papers there was the file on the "Courtney affair", with secret MI5 reports and letters. I had adapted the maxim of US presidential historian Robert Caro – "Turn every page" – and this time it worked.

Usually, the cloak of secrecy covers up most intelligence cases. Some MI5 files about World War II have been released to the National Archives, but the hidden hand of censorship in Whitehall is still being deployed.

When I researched the activities of Peter Smolka – a Soviet agent of influence in the early 1940s who was recruited by Kim Philby – many MI5 documents about his activities were available. But one key file is still being withheld because "it relates to the identity of a member of MI5". This MI5 officer is almost certainly dead unless he is more than 100 years old, so it is hard to understand the rationale behind such censorship.

Officially, government papers are released 30 years after the event. But some documents, including those relating to the sex security scandals involving John Profumo (1963) and

The hidden hand of censorship in Whitehall is still being deployed

CREDIT: PA/PA Archive/PA Images

ABOVE: Anthony Courtney, Harrow East MP
Conservative candidate, atop a loudspeaker
vehicle (left), alongside future British Prime
Minister Edward Heath, London, 1966

Lord Lambton (1973), remain under
lock and key. Despite the events in my
book taking place 40 to 60 years ago,
the culture of secrecy and the obstacles I
encountered remain.

Whitehall argues that sensitive
operational methods and sources will be
revealed by the release of MI5 and MI6
documents. These spies are long dead,

though, and operational methods have
changed dramatically since the Cold
War – especially with the greater focus
on technology for intelligence-gathering
and surveillance.

The security establishment claims it is
more transparent, but this is not the case
when it comes to the historical record
from which we can learn so much.

Looking back on his days as a KGB
officer, Russian president Vladimir Putin
said: "What amazed me most of all
was how one man's effort could achieve
what whole armies could not. How one

spy could decide the fate of thousands
of people."

Today, the role of intelligence is
paramount in Ukraine, so understanding
the KGB's past operations in the West
is vital – if the Whitehall weeders and
censors allow us. ✖

*Mark Hollingsworth is the author of Agents
of Influence – How the KGB Subverted
Western Democracies, which was published
this April by Oneworld*

52(03):90/91|DOI:10.1177/03064220231201320

First they came for the female journalists

Women are being erased from public life in Afghanistan. **ZAHRA JOYA** asks: Who will speak up for them if there are no female journalists left?

AFTER TWO DECADES of support from the international community and the establishment of a democratic system, journalism in Afghanistan had finally obtained a suitable platform for growth and development. More than 12,000 journalists and media workers were working; dozens of TV channels, hundreds of radio stations, newspapers and magazines were operating in different ways. Along with scientific and academic institutions, the media played an important role in shaping society's public culture, monitoring the government's functions and reflecting the people's wishes and demands.

Then the Taliban returned. It has been almost two years since the previous

ABOVE: Afghan journalist Zahra Joya

government fell, and the Taliban has taken over all government institutions. During this period, according to Reporters Without Borders, Afghanistan has fallen 34 places in terms of media freedom, and it is ranked 156th out of 180 countries.

The Taliban's Ministry of Propagation of Virtue and Prevention of Vice has banned female anchors and guests on the radio in most provinces, including Kandahar (the spiritual city of the Taliban). Female anchors, journalists and guests on television must cover their faces.

It seems now that suppressing free media and women is one of the main priorities of the Taliban and, by increasing pressure in various ways, it wants to disrupt the process of free information in society. Its hostility towards women has made the job for female journalists incredibly difficult. By imposing so many conditions, using intimidation and threats, and restricting movement, it has turned journalism into a forbidden job for them.

One example is the story of Shamima Ahadi. She has eight years of experience as a journalist but has now been forced to leave Afghanistan.

She told me: "One day in the Shahr-e-Naw area of Kabul, the Vice and Virtue guys stopped me and my friend. They harshly and threateningly criticised our way of dressing and hijab and finally said that we have no right to make a report without a male chaperone. When they approached us, their guns were in their hands, and they had put their fingers on the trigger. It was a very scary situation. My friend was crying and was in shock for a week."

Ahadi fled to Pakistan around a year ago. There, the situation has become even more difficult for her. She has

no place to stay and no way to leave, either. Economic problems combined with the risk of being arrested and then possibly sent back to Afghanistan have taken away her mental peace. Western countries and international organisations have largely turned their backs on female journalists and people like Ahadi.

Her story is common and representative of what many women journalists in Afghanistan face. Being a woman under the Taliban regime is a crime, and being a female journalist is a more serious one. By closing schools, universities and other educational centres to women, the process of educating and training a

When they approached us, their guns were in their hands, and they had put their fingers on the trigger

CREDIT: (Joya) Sandford St Martin Trust; (main) Abaca Press / Alamy

new generation of female journalists has stopped.

The continuation of this situation will remove women from journalism and turn this profession into a completely male one. According to the Taliban – and a very traditional section of society in Afghanistan – society does not need female journalists. But in their absence, how will the suffering of Afghan

women be reflected in the media? Can a completely male society understand women's issues? How can Afghan women's voices be covered in the health sector, education, the economy, work and politics? Who will represent them?

The international community and human rights organisations should not close their eyes to this bitter experience. Don't allow women to be removed from

ABOVE: Afghan women wait for donations of bread outside a Kabul bakery

the field of journalism. Don't allow women to be removed from public life. Ignoring the suffering of Afghan women and leaving them in the depths of Taliban darkness will have disastrous consequences; a disaster with a human burden that will weigh heavily on our consciences for generations to come. ✖

Zahra Joya is a journalist from Afghanistan and editor-in-chief of Rukhshana media

 Being a woman under the Taliban regime is a crime, and being a female journalist is a more serious one

52(03):92/93|DOI:10.1177/03064220231201321

GLOBAL VIEW

Speak, debate, challenge

Index's job is to report on all issues that undermine freedom of expression without fear or favour, writes **RUTH ANDERSON**

T SHOULD SURPRISE no one that I am profoundly committed to the basic human right of freedom of expression. After all, I run Index on Censorship. I have spent most of my adult life trying to provide a voice for people who struggle to be heard, and was brought up by an extraordinary woman who was adamant that those who had the skills and resources to fight for the rights of others had a moral requirement to do so. She taught me that campaigning for change and for a better society was the most important thing you could do with your life. And among the tools that we have to help people are our voices, which should be used as often as possible to demand change from those with the power to deliver it.

This led me to march against pit closures as a child, to campaign against neo-fascists as a teenager, to organise demos against factory closures in my 20s and to spend countless weekends campaigning for change in my community. Each of these pieces of activism has made me who I am, and I have been fortunate enough to live in a country where our right to speak up against injustice is largely free from fear of prosecution.

But while the concept of freedom of expression is straightforward and our rights to use it are protected in law, its application can be far from easy. Every issue that I have campaigned on has had an organised opposition, who have

exactly the same rights as me to campaign – as they should. In a democracy, the legal rights of my opponents are just as valuable as my own, even when I fundamentally disagree with them.

This is even more important when we consider identity and cultural change, because issues that touch people's personal lives are always emotive. This means the subject itself can become toxic and hurtful and can drive people away from seeking to understand the opposing viewpoints of the key protagonists. But as a political campaigner, I know that no argument or social debate has ever been resolved by fewer words, by less discussion – or by silence. Vital progressive battles are won by taking people on a journey, by persuading the moderate-middle that your cause is right, by being prepared to seek compromise, and by convincing politicians to take a stand. This was true for universal suffrage, for the civil rights movement, for abortion rights and for gay marriage – and it will likely be true for every cultural change that will happen in my lifetime going forward.

That doesn't mean that having these debates is easy. As a member of a minority community, I know how painful it can be to watch other people debate your identity and your rights. I know how frustrating it is to watch others pontificate about what's best for you and your community – or worse, why you're wrong and others are right. I've

had too much experience of where some of these debates can lead to and of where challenging language can become abuse and then threats. But that doesn't make freedom of expression a less important right, or one that we should renege upon.

This brings me to the one issue that seems to dominate every conversation I have about my work at the moment – gender identity. Current conversations are all too often toxic. Every discussion brings hurt and anger. I've sat with friends as they've cried over the fear they face because of the personal and aggressive nature of the current discourse and I've spoken to dozens of people who feel isolated and are self-censoring as they don't want to get caught in the maelstrom.

All of which brings me to the role of Index.

Index is not, and will never be, a campaign vehicle for any issue other than the protection and promotion of freedom of expression as a democratic human right. We exist solely to protect and promote this right around the world – not to pick a side on an issue of conscience and of personal values. Our job is to report on issues which undermine freedom of expression without fear or favour, and to provide a platform for those people who are persecuted. While our professional staff and our board may all have their own opinions, institutionally we are not – and we will not be – aligned with any organisation that seeks to silence opposing views.

Within this context I think it is vitally important to restate our approach to freedom of expression.

This is our guiding framework for freedom of expression:

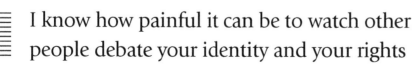

I know how painful it can be to watch other people debate your identity and your rights

Index on Censorship applies a consistent approach to freedom of expression across all of our work streams. In line with Article 10 of the European Convention on Human Rights we promote and protect the fundamental human right of freedom of expression, but we will not defend hate speech or incitement to violence as defined currently under the law.

This means that we will always focus our efforts to defend the rights of dissidents, academics, journalists and campaigners – amongst others – to speak, argue, debate, challenge and campaign.

Index on Censorship's remit is and always has been global. The threats we therefore respond to are varied, but we respond to all. Today trans voices top the lists of books banned at libraries and schools across the USA, while in the UK we have seen repeated attempts to prevent gender-critical feminists from exercising their lawful rights to speech. We will and do oppose both.

Index defends the right of people to speak, but that is not the same as the right to be heard. These are different things. No one has the right for their views to be heard on any given platform and to be accepted by the wider world. At the same time, we oppose the cancelling and silencing of voices associated with a specific view. We will defend the rights of people to speak if they have been invited, and in turn we defend the rights of those who seek to peacefully protest views that they don't share. These are all different issues and the nuances are important here.

Index believes that state institutions funded by the tax payer, such as the BBC, have a responsibility to represent a range of viewpoints and we will challenge them if we believe they are falling short of that responsibility. But that does not mean always giving equal weight to a selection of views – that is an editorial decision. Nor do the same responsibilities apply to private and/or voluntary bodies. If the latter chose to not print a certain viewpoint we won't automatically assume that's censorship and instead will investigate further.

As with all issues that shape both democratic and authoritarian societies, we will provide editorial comment highlighting where people's freedom of expression is restricted because of their views, and we will report on this without fear or favour.

Index's commitment to freedom of expression on every issue is unwavering – and has been since our founding in 1972. We were established to provide a platform for the persecuted and to protect freedom of expression at home, regardless of how controversial or unpopular a voice may be. It is not for us to judge which voices need to be heard; only for us to highlight which voices are being silenced and campaign for a world in which censorship does not exist. ✖

Ruth Anderson is CEO of Index

52(03):94/95|DOI:10.1177/03064220231201322

CULTURE

"I realised that here was the kernel for a story, a novel, in fact, in which someone starts to murder the refugees in an Embassy like the one I inhabited"

ARIEL DORFMAN | THE EMBASSY MURDERS | P.99

Will Paulina ever rest?

ARIEL DORFMAN tells **JEMIMAH STEINFELD** why his fictional character must raise her voice once more, in his new short story for Index

CELEBRATED CHILEAN-AMERICAN PLAYWRIGHT and author Ariel Dorfman yearns for the day his play, Death and the Maiden, is no longer relevant. Until then the play's central character Paulina will continue to haunt him, and indeed us.

"She resonates magnificently, sorrowfully, accusingly, and will do so for, alas, a long time, until she can rest, until a day comes when spectators will leave the theatre asking: 'Torture? What is torture? Can any society really have condoned such violence? It must be something the author invented'," Dorfman told Index.

For the unacquainted, Death and the Maiden, which was originally published in Index and later turned into a film by Roman Polanski, follows Paulina Escobar, a former political prisoner from an undetermined place, who was raped and tortured by her captors (led by a sadistic doctor). Years later, after the repressive regime has fallen, Paulina is convinced that she has finally found the man responsible and the story follows her quest for revenge.

But Paulina is not just a character from Death and the Maiden. She is now a character in The Embassy Murders, Ariel Dorfman's new short story published

exclusively here for the first time. So why does she keep on coming back? As Dorfman says, she's never really left him since he conceived her back in 1990 because the situation that gave rise to her – justice unfulfilled – continues.

"If Chile had been able to afford her and so many others some justice once the dictatorship had been defeated, she would not have been forced to seek justice on her own and I would not have been forced to write the words she seemed to be dictating to me. But Chile, like most lands that have suffered terrible atrocities and need to move forward and not be trapped in the past, was unable to repair her wounds or assuage her grief," he said.

Worst still, today in Chile Augusto Pinochet's coup and the resulting dictatorship is the subject of positive revisionism, said Dorfman (see also pg…). Rather than a consensus from left to right condemning his reign of terror, "extreme right-wing sectors, encouraged by recent electoral victories, have declared that they justify the military takeover — and many of them flirt with denial that such violations even occurred," he said, adding:

"This position is extremely dangerous because of what these people are implying: if you ever try to change Chile again as you did in the Allende years, we will come after you again and this time, as the joke goes, "No more Mister Nice-Guy". And this at a moment when the trust in democracy is eroding, both in Chile and all over the world."

Dorfman said "it is up to the citizens of Chile to isolate those anti-democratic elements and make them irrelevant."

The central plot of The Embassy Murders is compelling. It's set between 1973, when 1,000 people are crammed into Santiago's Argentinian Embassy seeking refuge for their role in resisting the coup, and the early 1990s, when Dorfman is wrestling with his return to Chile and what to do with literary

characters that he has abandoned. He toys with the idea of penning a story about a psychopathic killer on the loose in the embassy in 1973. The result is "an embodiment of the metaverse, an alternative way in which certain events could have occurred in a parallel universe", he said.

Dorfman himself sought refuge in the embassy in 1973, an experience that he unsurprisingly calls "unforgettable" and that he has written about in detail often. He has also visited the embassy since and tells Index of three particular times. In one, he went with the daughter of the young revolutionary Sergio Leiva, who had been shot and killed on 3 January 1974 by snipers from one of the adjacent apartment complexes. For him the anecdote "gives a sense of the dread we felt while we were there, how death surrounded us and finally targeted one of the refugees". In another, when having dinner with his wife Angélica, he was amused when the ambassador's wife asked if he needed directions to the bathroom.

"I laughed. 'No, I went to that bathroom many times during weeks and weeks. Except on this occasion there will not be a line of 50 or 60 men waiting their turn outside'."

A third visit, this year, saw him eat at the very spot he had once slept (under a billiard table).

"The exquisite meal our hosts prepared for us made the visit even more surreal because I had gone hungry often when I was in that embassy (not easy to feed 1,000 refugees)," he said.

> Torture? What is torture? Can any society really have condoned such violence?

Death surrounded us and finally targeted one of the refugees

Back to Paulina. Can she be put to rest? While Dorfman says there are Paulinas all over the world, at least when it comes to Chile people can try to ensure a reckoning with their own Paulinas.

"We just have to keep on telling the truth and hope that the seeds find fertile ground. My novel, The Suicide Museum, which inspired me to write The Embassy Murders story, has been my way of contributing to establishing that painful truth."

Jemimah Steinfeld is editor-in-chief at Index

The Embassy Murders

By ARIEL DORFMAN

S THERE A place where unfinished characters go to die, go to wait for a resurrection that, in most cases, never comes?

* * *

When I returned to Chile after seventeen years of exile, I brought home with me the initial pages of a novel, *The Embassy Murders*, that I had carried with me all through my wanderings and that I now intended to continue and complete.

I had started it, oh so tentatively, one lucid night (or was it a drab afternoon?), sometime in the autumn of 1973 in the Argentine Embassy in Santiago, where I had sought refuge after the coup that toppled the democratically elected President of Chile, Salvador Allende. It was one of the only safe places in the country, thanks to a principle, the *"derecho de asilo"*, that had been established in 19th century Latin America during the turmoil and civil wars that had followed Independence as a way of preserving the lives of the elites from warring factions that went in and out of the revolving doors of each shifting regime.

I had been working at the Presidential Palace during the last months of our revolutionary government and, having narrowly escaped the death that had come for Allende himself during the September 11th military takeover, I had gone on the run for several weeks, constantly changing safe houses, one step ahead of General Pinochet's secret police, until I reluctantly accepted to be smuggled into the grounds of the enormous Argentine Ambassador's residence in central Santiago. But barely enormous enough to lodge the thousand and more refugees from all over the continent jammed into salons which, only recently, had hosted urbane diplomats and glittering guests imbibing champagne and canapés.

I would never, in those congested circumstances, pressed on all sides by sweaty, fearful, desperate bodies, have conceived the impractical notion of writing something as civilised as a novel if someone had not dropped in on me – literally – from the sky one evening in late October.

I was walking in the ample gardens of the embassy. I liked that twilight time of day, when I could find some solitude far from innumerable bickering revolutionaries who, at most other hours, crowded the lawn and trampled the flowers, barely dodging children who ran by screaming slogans. We called them los termitas, a horde of youngsters whose parents could not control them any more than they could control their own depression and anxiety. I savoured the chance of breathing some fresh air and pursuing the brooding questions of how the hell could our peaceful revolution have ended up so disastrously, what the hell did we do wrong, how to make sure we did not repeat the same mistakes again. If there was ever to be an again.

And then, as if heaven had decided to answer those questions, well, not really answer them, merely interrupt them, a bundle fell at my feet, flung over the colossal back wall of the embassy. I heard shots from the other side—the police were constantly patrolling the perimeter of that building, trying to catch anyone endeavoring to sneak in—and then, quickly, miraculously, a   →

➔ body came over the wall, the man rolled in the grass like one of those muscular movie heroes parachuting behind enemy lines. He stood up and peered nearsightedly at me, picked up the bundle and adjusted a pair of glasses on his nose and grinned, said, "Ah! Ariel! Never thought we'd meet again like this, eh? But, hey, I had nobody to beat at chess, so why not pay you a visit?"

It was Abel Balmaceda, a former mate at the University, a member of an extreme left-wing group that believed that armed struggle was the only way to get rid of the dictatorship.

He only wanted to stay the night, by no means register with the embassy functionaries, he'd be gone once he'd delivered a message to an unnamed person who had sought asylum, could I find a way to hide him for the night?

No problem. I had been feeling sick lately and lucky enough to be treated by our family doctor, Daniel Vaisman, who was himself a refugee at the embassy. Danny had convinced his fellow physicians to let me sleep under the billiards table of the recreation room they had requisitioned as their medical headquarters. With their connivance, Abel could be concealed in that haven until he had unobtrusively carried out his mission.

We spent the whole night arguing over tactics and the future and who was to blame for the defeat of Allende's revolution – militants like me who were too peaceful and wanted to advance too slowly or militants like Abel who were too violent and wanted to advance too rapidly. We reached, of course, no agreement before he left the next day, having completed whatever task he had been assigned, but he did accomplish, without meaning to, something else.

I had considered the Embassy as a sanctuary, the only dwelling in a country gone mad, where death could not reach me. But if Abel had managed to enter and leave the Embassy with such ease, was it not conceivable - and even likely – that someone else, with less benign intentions, might do something similar, what if some agent of the Junta was planning to leap over the wall. Wait! What if some perverse criminal had already done so, was among us at that moment. Worse

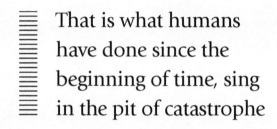

That is what humans have done since the beginning of time, sing in the pit of catastrophe

still. What if he had not needed to leap over anything, had sought asylum as I had? What if we were in danger?

I dismissed these fears as paranoid and yet, the disquiet I felt continued to churn in my sleepless mind until, suddenly, I realised that here was the kernel for a story, a novel, in fact, in which someone starts to murder the refugees in an Embassy like the one I inhabited. An extraordinary, juicy set up. A thousand prospective victims and a thousand possible suspects and nobody to solve the case or, yes, cases, as the bodies piled up. A horror story: all of us here, being stalked by a mysterious killer, while outside on the streets millions of others were also being stalked by other kinds of killers, far less mysterious and more lethal. No, not a horror story. A detective story. The Chilean police could not investigate due the Embassy's extraterritoriality, but someone among the asylum seekers could do so, someone who had the skills of the best sort of investigator, someone who – that was it, an ace detective from *Investigaciones*, the Chilean FBI, who had fallen in love with some wild revolutionary woman and snuck her into the Embassy and then stayed on, leaving wife and child behind, and was now the only one who could solve the murders, perhaps even save his lover who might be the next target.

It might seem frivolous to be spinning this sort of tale, even its possibility, in such dire moments, with so much real terror and real bodies being hunted down, but that is what humans have done since the beginning of time, sing in the pit of catastrophe, tell stories that make sense or at least offer some consolation and reprieve as our house burns down. To be creative in such circumstances is a way of defying the extinction that threatens to make everything absurd and transient, proof that we are still alive as every dream is shattered into pieces by military boots.

And, after all, I might as well put the long confinement ahead to good use. My models would be Cervantes and Boethius, Oscar Wilde and Solzhenitsyn, Jean Genet and Ezra Pound, prisoners all through history - and this was a benevolent version of prison - who had written to stay sane, had turned their misfortune into an occasion to deepen their understanding of our finite bodies and our infinite imagination.

I contacted the diplomat in charge of our welfare, a man called Neumann, who made no effort to hide his fascist sympathies, his defense of the coup as necessary. He was a cruel man, always shrugging his shoulders when asked for anything out of the ordinary, seeming to delight in our powerlessness, that we were under his control and he could do – well, almost – anything he wanted with us, humiliate us, despise us, suggest we were cowards for not having stayed to face the consequences of our irresponsible revolution.

I had taken an instant dislike to him the afternoon that I clambered out of the trunk of the diplomatic car that had escorted me into the Embassy and introduced himself, not deigning to shake my hand, brushing it aside as if it were some sort of bothersome rodent. Angular, with eyes like rusty hinges and hair to match, as if caked with dirty carrots, he had emphasised that his name was Neumann with two ns, said this twice, not like Dorfman, he said, not Jewish, he meant. Nor did he get any more pleasant as the days dragged by, days and then weeks and finally months under his tutelage. He had even mistreated my wife Angélica when she had come to inquire at the Consulate if I needed anything, food, a blanket, a change of underwear. That's not my problem, he said to her. He's the one who chose to leave his family and seek safety with us. He's safe, that should be enough for you.

So, consumed as I was by the creative bug, I hesitated before telling him I'd appreciate it if he could provide me with a ballpoint pen, some paper. In my favour: I had already wangled from him, the week before, a copy of Don Quixote. He

had objected – what a suspicious bastard! - why did I need that novel by Cervantes, as if there were something subversive that could be hidden in the pages about the sad knight of La Mancha, but I had convinced him that, with the book in hand, I could read and explain it to my fellow refugees, choose the most restless and aggressive ones and use the greatest novel in the world to calm them down, dream of windmills rather than going on a hunger strike if the Embassy did not accept their demands. And now? Neumann said. Now you need paper, a pen? Why?

And I lied, naturally: To prepare my classes, I replied. To make sure what I say has a soothing effect on my militant students.

Some hours later, he reluctantly forked over a ballpoint pen and two sheets of paper. But that's it, no more than this, he said. We're way over budget. You people eat as if it were the last day of your lives.

I didn't respond that we had feared, still feared, for our lives, that all of us had thought at some point, this is the last day of my life – I had felt that way since the coup and, as for the array of Latin Americans from all the countries across the continent, they had been hounded, jailed, tortured, did not know if the meal they were eating was, in effect, their last one – I said nothing of this to Neumann, merely thanked him, and rushed off to see if I could find some corner that was solitary enough to scribble what was racing through my mind. I tried to distract myself from a discussion between a former Brazilian senator with an Uruguayan Tupamaro as to whether it made sense to kidnap and execute their enemies who had engaged in repression in their respective states, or if that sort of action was always counterproductive, allowing revolutionaries to be painted as terrorists. As they focused on the case of a CIA agent in Montevideo who had come to teach the police how to torture, the conversation grew convoluted and strident, vexing me, and I wondered, vindictively, if I should not choose one of these two contestants to be the first victim in my book, that would at least silence them fictitiously – and the thought helped me to stagger on and come up with....   ➔

→   I sat down to impatiently write the first pages of the saga – my detective's name would be Antonio Coloma and he would be the narrator of this mystery.

* * *

The question remains and returns: is there a place where unfinished characters go to die, go to wait for a resurrection that, in most cases, never comes?

Unfinished characters: not the ones who are given the chance to die in the pages of the novel or play or story or epic poem, not the ones offered a rounded-off demise by their author. I don't mean Anna Karenina or Emma Bovary or old man Karamazov or Aschenbach or Ivan Illyich or Pere Goriot or K., poor K.

I mean the ones we have never heard of because their makers left them half complete – or one third or one fifth or one twenty-fifth complete - deserted midway (if they are lucky to even have made it that far) through their journey. Or maybe fire consumed the pages of their lives and they remained barely more than ashes, a smoldering heap, not even offered the surcease of being kept in a forgotten drawer to be thrown out as garbage, the man or woman who afforded them with a frail, precarious existence passed away, taking with her, with him, the mendacious pledge of a potential renewal.

So forgotten that they only exist in this moment when I imagine that multitude of invented human characters, some of them seething, others suspended in the dark, ears attuned to the living, still lighting themselves up with a hope, however faint, of receiving closure.

Others, I presume, have given up hope a long time ago.

Or do the unfinished always remain somewhere, in the expectation that a hand will reach out to rescue them from oblivion, reach out to ink and paper or a keyboard or a recording machine of some sort or even someone telling their story around a campfire.

* * *

A few hours later, the sheets of paper were covered with words, an opening salvo narrated by Antonio Coloma:

I was waiting to take a piss that dawn—there were twenty-six refugees ahead of me—when I was told that there had been a murder at the embassy. And that my services as a former chief inspector would be required, as the local police were forbidden from intervening.
My bladder was about to burst.

I cursed it, cursed having overslept, cursed the men who were closer to urinating than I was, cursed the men behind me who would take my hard-earned place in line if I left to attend to a crime that really should not concern me, cursed that I was here in this embassy crammed in with a thousand souls—or, rather, their smelly, stinking, sweating, frightened, constipated bodies—cursed their armpits, groins, fingers, infected feet and bloated stomachs, and sex, above all I cursed their sex and their pleasure when I was getting so little of either, I cursed that I could no longer pull out a police badge and shove aside the other candidates for the urinals and exert my privileges over the rest of mankind, I cursed everything but the love that had led me to abandon my boring wife of ten years and my anodyne child of nine and seek refuge here after the coup to accompany the woman of my dreams into exile.
But enough curses. The Argentine embassy's chargé d'affaires had crept up to my side to urge me to examine the corpse that had been stabbed during the night, so I turned to him and said: "I'll only help if you find me a bathroom first."

And that was as far as I got.

For two reasons.

The first: I ran out of paper. And doubted that Neumann would provide more.

And the second: I realised that the time had inevitably come to give a name, a face to the corpse, some comrade I had come to love or probably to detest, had to model my victim on someone close to me and then kill him or her off. As if that weren't enough, other troubles were brewing for my novel. In order to find the murderer, Coloma would be forced to examine possible motives behind the killing, scrutinise

an array of suspects from a wide spectrum of revolutionary movements, steering his way through the history of frustrated dreams and unrealised utopias milling around the Embassy grounds. He could not discover the culprit without delving into the petty and substantial squabbles between militants, the ways in which the victim (and there would be more, several more at least) had sided with this or that faction, this or that theory, a continent seething with failed attempts to change society, oh yes, my detective could not avoid scrounging into the glory and garbage of the kind of circular discussions about strategy that led nowhere that I had just had with Abel Balmaceda under the billiard table: recriminations, differences about how to create a coalition with the middle classes, how to confront the dictatorship now, through armed struggle or through a renewed belief in democracy, and

what to do with the indigenous population, and what was the role of women, and were peasants reactionary or natural allies of industrial workers, we can't repeat failed experiments of the past, you're to blame, no, you are.

Was this really the time to *sacar nuestros trapos al sol*, reveal all our blemishes and frailties? When we were trying to recover from the worst defeat of the left in the history of Chile and a terrible catastrophe for all progressive forces worldwide? Was it our bickering and reproaches that we wanted to exhibit, giving ammunition to our foes? If we were unable to agree among ourselves on how best to confront the dictatorship how could we pretend to ever again govern a land we had led to this disaster?

No, this was not the novel we needed when the house was burning down.

I abandoned it.   →

✦   * * *

It is unlikely that there are guards at the border of the Land of the Unfinished, no visas required, no passports other than the lack of completion, no customs officers to find out if somebody is smuggling anything illegal in – and it would be a waste of resources to have anyone stopping the homeless expatriates (for that is what they all are, that country is a huge refugee camp filled with exiles and forced evacuees) from departing, they are stuck, stagnating there, without any need of policing other than their own eternally migrant, eternally transient condition.

Perhaps, as in all human societies, there is a hierarchy, established from the start by those who had the misfortune – they might argue the privilege – of having been among the first of the unwritten, semi-heroes from hieroglyphic communities, but even if that were not the case, some of the characters would probably claim some kind of pre-eminence: we are less unfinished than you are, those who merited only a few lines and then were discarded should have less say in how we run our affairs, I was part of an epic battle (alas, it lacked the culminating scene), you are no more than the figment of an inconclusive domestic romance, our writer is still alive and may come back for us, your writer has been buried many eons ago, but perhaps these characters have overcome the ruthless politics of the world of their authors and cohabitate peacefully with one another, the only human place (other than death?) where the utopia of equality has ever fully materialised.

Who knows?

Catastrophes bring out the worst in us and our creatures.

And the best, of course.

* * *

Yes, I abandoned the novel, but whispered to Coloma: I'll be back, you're not dead, only waiting for the right moment to be revived. Proof that I meant that promise: I did not throw away those pages when I left the embassy in mid-December of 1973, kept them in some nearby drawer all through the years that followed, dormant, not forgotten, I even managed at some point to figure out a bit more of the backstory of my brilliant police inspector. I decided that he had arrested a femme fatale some days before the coup, for illegally carrying a gun, ostensibly in defense of a revolution that was already foundering, though it would be my Antonio Coloma who had foundered, lost himself in the guiles and curves and oceanic eyes of that embodiment of Bizet's Carmen, explored every inch of her body during nights of unbridled sex. And when the military takeover endangered that revolutionary seductress, he had smuggled her into the embassy and had been unable to resist the temptation of staying by her side. Forsaking family and vocation, so that instead of investigating some homicide in a remote neighbourhood of Santiago, or capturing the serial killer he'd been tracking down for the last year, he found himself, thanks to a mistaken and perhaps morbid infatuation, stuck in a building full of people he knew very little about, representatives of every oppressed nation in Latin America.

And as the Pinochet dictatorship, ever more unpopular, weakened by mass protests and internal dissension, was forced to give way to the rule of the people and my own return to my country, as I began to contemplate what I would write upon that return, it was my Embassy Murders novel that increasingly occupied he forefront of my mind. With Pinochet gone, I could finally try to answer, at least in a fictional excursion, the questions I had postponed during my years of banishment: How could we not have seen this catastrophe and therefore avoided it? How responsible are each of us for having led so many to be slaughtered, how responsible are we for having promised them paradise and led them to hell?

Yes, a restored democracy allowed me, I thought, to face, through the multiple inhabitants of the embassy, the transgressions and mistakes of the left in Chile and Latin America, the sort of critique that I had not allowed myself to express publicly during the years of dictatorship, for fear of how our enemies would use my words against the cause of revolution I still believed in.

And thus, when I went back to newly democratic Chile in 1990, I brought with me Antonio Coloma and his lover Rachael – yes, she would be Jewish - and all those refugees who, in my novel, would soon be subjected to the murderous eyes and hands of an as yet undetermined killer.

* * *

When the cancelled characters were exiled to the Land of the Unfinished I conceive them as being greeted by who knows how many others sharing their plight, like souls in Purgatory who, forbidden for the moment from ascending to Heaven and celestial enlightenment, nurse the consolation that at least they are not in Limbo, have not been consigned to the condition of not having been born at all. Yes, they must be telling themselves there is hope, even as each hour, each day and month and year brings nearer the risk of forgetfulness, oh, they cling to their half-shaped identity, praying that they will be remembered.

* * *

Things had not gone as I had planned. Not with the novel, not with my return.

A month after I had settled in with my wife and two boys, a novelist friend, a man of refinement and culture, had asked: "So...How has Ithaca been treating you?"

He must have noticed something in my eyes at his question, a flicker of alarm or maybe puzzlement, maybe he realised that until then I had kept to myself what I had been feeling, whatever he realised, he nevertheless did not relent: "Your homecoming. All those mythical tales contain a truth, a yearning that is deep inside us. Of course, Odysseus was gone twenty years, and for you it's been seventeen, but still, there must be parallels. Some semblance of Ithaca awaits us all. And some of us go home and some of us don't."

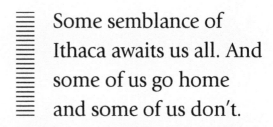

Some semblance of Ithaca awaits us all. And some of us go home and some of us don't.

How had Ithaca been treating me?

I suddenly felt the urge to express my experience over the last month.

"Ithaca?" I blurted the name out as if it were an insult rather than a mythical destination, and merely articulating it so explosively, with such anger and bitterness, let loose the floodgates of my emotion. "Well, Odysseus, before he could take possession of the home he'd lost, had to deal with the suitors. There's a reason why they're part of that epic. It tells us that you can't go home, completely recuperate it, until you've faced those who seized and soiled that home. In our case, we decided not to slay them, the right decision, though less a decision than a fait accompli, as our enemies were the ones who had done the slaying, they raped Penelope during our absence, tore to shreds the wedding dress she was weaving by day and unweaving by night. If The Odyssey had been true to reality rather than the projection of a dream, it would have shown how Odysseus was betrayed and massacred by the suitors before he even had a chance to shoot off one arrow from his legendary bow. Because our reality, the reality of Chile, taught us that the suitors couldn't be defeated with violence, so if we wanted our land and our rights back, we'd have to cohabitate with them. And leave those usurpers all the booty accumulated during the years we were away, and I'm not talking only of the ones who had to physically leave the country. Even those who remained behind were exiles, maybe more painful for them because they had to witness the violations every minute without protesting, like those of us who were outside the country could. So in our Chilean Ithaca, our enemies kept what they plundered, the farms, the newspapers, the factories, the malls, the army, the navy, the air   →

An unknown murderer is trying to undermine the safety that someone like you created

➔ force, the police, and the courts of so-called justice, and allowed us to vote and say what we wanted as long as we did not want too much, say what was on our mind as long as we did not say everything that was on our mind, as long as we don't threaten to take back the riches and brides they've stolen."

"All of which," my friend observed mildly, "was part of the pact we signed, the price you and I and those who were defeated when Allende died, what we had to pay."

I nodded. "No complaining," I said. "Tolerable, given that we were the losers in this game— tolerable as long as . . . as long as . . ."

And I did not go on. Because I was about to venture into forbidden territory. I had thus far framed this excoriation of Ithaca as a collective tragedy and had kept my individual experience out of it, but what I would have gone on to say now would have been too nakedly revelatory. I had been on the verge of saying that the price paid was tolerable as long as we, as long as I, entertained the belief that Penelope was indeed awaiting us, awaiting me, as she had waited for her husband. It had been the law of hospitality that had kept him alive abroad and that saved me during my own years of wandering and it was that law I expected would now be enacted and fulfilled when we returned. But now, in the place I had always thought of as home, as our Ithaca, it was not hospitality but hostility or, worse than that, indifference that greeted us. There was no Penelope who was true to me, no matter how much people rapturously claimed to have missed us. There were exceptions, of course, our immediate family and some friends like this novelist who had greeted me like a long-lost child, but most of those in the cultural and political

elite seemed to resent my return or had simply ignored my presence, did not call back when I left messages, did not invite me to their gatherings. The worst experiences had been at a couple of book launches that I had attended despite a very pointed lack of an invitation. My wife Angélica had refused to go—"If they don't want you, then don't show up"—but I had insisted and had been greeted coldly or with feigned warmth by several of the authors to whom I had sent funds, the very ones who had thanked me in the past for helping them to stay in Chile rather than emigrate as I had done. This studied, spiteful, everyday lack of recognition was particularly agonising because it embodied for me something more serious, that I did not recognise this country as mine anymore, that too much had changed, in me or in Chile itself, to make this return comfortable, as welcoming as I had dreamt it all through my years abroad. I did not say any of this to my novelist friend because I did not wish to admit all that the people of my country had lost during these years of internal and external banishment.

If the novel had gone well I might have ignored this estrangement, because it would have been a sign of how relevant I was despite the contempt and neglect with which I was being greeted, I would have used it to batter down the walls of indifference with which I was mistreated, force the country (or at least the most prominent members of its intelligentsia) to acknowledge my importance, my contribution to the transition to democracy by asking hard questions about yesterday but also about the situation today. After all, the murderer in the embassy was merely anticipating what the secret police would do under Pinochet with State support. The difference was that I intended my detective to nab the culprit whereas the serial killers of Allende supporters roamed the streets of contemporary Chile without having ever been identified, caught and judged. So my work of fiction, conceived so long ago inside that one place exempt from the widespread State violence engulfing the country, was a way of imposing at least some form of justice, albeit literary, so absent from today's real Chile, just as it had been absent during the dictatorship.

Alas, I had been unable to advance beyond those words I had scribbled years ago on the paper I had managed to finagle out of the dreadful Neumann. The remote possibility occurred to me that this persistent blockage might be due to the fact that this was not what I needed to write – or what the country, for that matter, needed from me. But I dismissed that idea. No, I had promised Antonio Coloma that I would not disown him. Feeling betrayed myself, how could I betray him? No, what was stopping me, I thought, was that I did not know enough about how the embassy functioned officially. Seventeen years had passed and it was indispensable to do some research. My own limited experience while there was insufficient, I had to feed my imagination with some real facts.

The first person I wanted to contact was Félix Córdoba Moyano, the diplomat who had done the most to insure my safety and that of the other refugees, tirelessly rescuing tortured prisoners from the National Stadium, seeking out more ways to fit more people into the increasingly reduced halls of the embassy, sparring with the authorities who denied us safe-conducts. He had become such a pain in the ass to the junta that a formal protest had been lodged with the increasingly right-wing Argentine government, a pressure that had eventually led to Félix's banishment to the bleakest diplomatic posts, first Thailand, then Nigeria, ultimately Albania. His purgatory was only now ending with a deployment to the United Nations in New York, where I managed to track him down – delighted that neither his voice nor his convictions had not changed over the years.

I explained the basic plot of my novel: "An unknown murderer is trying to undermine the safety that someone like you created for those refugees, taking lives that you saved, reversing the work you did." But the premise I was playing with depended on the certainty that, if there had been a murder, and the Chilean government had demanded that the first corpse (and then the next ones) be handed over to the proper authorities, subjected to an autopsy and bureaucratic procedures, the Argentinians,

backed by the whole diplomatic corps, would have adamantly refused. So the Chilean police would lack clues, fingerprints, search warrants, and interrogations. And what about the bodies, would they be stored in a freezer until the impasse of who controlled them had been settled, or would they have been turned over at some point (and when?) to the proper authorities? Even if forensic experts eventually received a body, the judge and detectives still would be unable to ascertain the circumstances of the crime scene, or motives and alibis of possible perpetrators among the thousand and one refugees, Hercule Poirot himself could not have whittled such hordes down to a manageable list. The limitations an official investigator faced in such an explosive situation, I continued, were apparently insurmountable, a literary challenge I looked forward to solving. But I could not do it without more information. Would he help me do justice to his experience and mine?

For the next hour or so – I ran up quite a phone bill but it was worth it – Félix poured a torrent of details into my ears, a list of potential victims and suspects, whether a fight over jurisdiction really could have led to a war between the two countries. Also, how all personnel that came in and out of the embassy were screened, ways in which those applying for asylum were vetted to make sure no agent of the armed forces infiltrated the premises, methods used to avoid precisely the sort of drastic situation my fictitious detective was investigating. And he told me stories he had collected from the refugees—the Tupamaro Uruguayans who had been part of the operation that had killed the CIA agent Dan Mitrione in Montevideo; the Guatemalans who had resisted the invasion that had toppled the democratic government of Arbenz; the Salvadoran woman who had lost two brothers in the insurrection against the banana companies; the Colombian who had been with the revolutionary priest Camilo Torres when he was killed, and the Bolivian communists who had been accused of not assisting Che Guevara in his hour of need; the Brazilians who had demanded samba music or they'd go on a hunger strike; the Dominicans   →

→ and Venezuelans and Paraguayans, all of Latin America was represented in that embassy, the thwarted hopes and warped aspirations of a whole continent. Not to forget the crazy Argentinians. There was one who had falsely boasted in his Chilean shantytown that he was an expert at making bombs, hoping to impress a young and spicy ultra-revolutionary girl who was secretly a police informant. Picked up by soldiers the day after the coup and dispatched to the National Stadium, he had spent tearful hours trying to convince his tormentors that he had made it all up, I did it for love, he would scream, I did it because I wanted that girl to admire me so I could give her a good poke.

I asked him about a series of other issues. How had the embassy staff dealt with the scarcity of food and bedding, the myriad strategies to sneak people into the premises. He told me that many had initially done so through the adjoining Consulate, pretending they needed some document stamped, a tactic that hadn't lasted much, as the Carabineros guarding the door began to discern that many of those entering the Consulate never emerged from it. So much that I learned from him that I had failed to absorb while I was there.

Félix's account inspired me to persevere in my inquiries.

Next up was Dr. Danny Vaisman who had returned from his own exile and was happy to contribute to my novel. I found out from him how a corpse would be handled if a murder had unmistakably been committed. And there would be more murders, so where did he and his colleagues store their medical supplies, and who had access to them? Was there any poison? How soon would they realise if a potentially lethal

I did it because I wanted that girl to admire me so I could give her a good poke

drug was missing? Did they keep a record of the patients? Could that record have been stolen? And the surgical instruments, the scalpels, where were they kept? Were any of the doctors present equipped to carry out an autopsy? What sort of implements were available, and who could provide them among the embassy staff? Would they be in touch with the Santiago morgue and its forensic specialists? How would they preserve the body until the parties disputing it had wrangled out jurisdiction?

Inspired by those reams of facts – and by other stories I garnered from fellow refugees I spoke to at length – I returned to my interrupted literary endeavor, to Antonio Coloma waiting to take a piss in the ashen dawn of that embassy.

* * *

The derelict characters send messages across the divide, the ever-winding abyss that their creators are not aware of, they send messages that are seldom answered or even acknowledged. But once in a while one of them is plucked from the fields of the Unfinished and brought into the room or garden or beach where their newly inspired author abides, and that character so selected will not again be left to wither on the shores of laziness and indifference or mere lack of inspiration or funds. But they are the exception. There are always far more half-formed figments of the imagination pouring into the Land of the Unfinished than the few who depart in dribbles. Though those few exercise a powerful influence upon those who remain: Edwin Drood, for instance, is the stuff of legends, his fate a constant source of the possibility of redemption by someone other than the original author. Wasn't his story, left undeveloped by Dickens when he died, taken up by many others? To point out that the vast majority of these inchoate and deficient legions were not devised by anyone famous or commercial enough to warrant such special treatment would be useless. And cruel. Why make their existence any more miserable, take from them the crumbs and dregs of hope?

* * *

So what came next in my novel?

Did I take a chronological leap and go straight to the victim? Or concentrate on the pissing itself and Coloma's view of his own penis and where it had led him, how he had not made love for a while to Rachael, the woman who had brought him to that embassy? Or maybe shift the point of view to the murderer, in italics, some bilious thoughts that wouldn't identify him but offer a glimpse of what my detective was up against? Or should I focus on the *chargé d'affaires* pleading for Coloma's help, would he be someone who assisted or obstructed, should I inveigle readers into being suspicious of him or were there, in fact, reasons to harbour suspicions about what that man's true motives might be. Or . . . or . . . or . . .

Too many alternatives, and none of them grabbed me by the throat, propelled me toward

what should immediately follow. Maybe something erotic? Death and sex, what better combination to entice the reader?

I concentrated on Rachael and Antonio, the difficulties for them to make love when there were hundreds of eavesdropping neighbours suffering from insomnia and loneliness and envy in the near vicinity, when would this impossibility of coupling begin to wear down their relationship, could love persist for Coloma—or for her, for her—if there was no sex?

What was certain was that they would be clutching at the memories of their first torrid rapport, those few brief, already fading, days when their bodies had fused together, before the coup had disrupted their chance to confirm whether this relationship could go beyond a mere series of perfectly coordinated orgasms. Was it only something physical, and therefore transitory, that united them? Coloma and Rachael could ➔

→ hear others nearby, couples attempting intimacy under frayed blankets and inside half-open closets, but those sighs and grunts, those gasps of urging and wonder and discharge dampened their ardour, I decided that no matter how much she rubbed his genitals and he groped toward her clitoris, it was inadequate —and the mutilated corpse that was to take centre stage in that embassy would only hasten the instant when one of them would admit that this had all been a mistake, that they were ill-suited for one another over the long-haul, she would go into exile without him, he had sacrificed his life, lost his land and his job, his wife and kid, without the compensation of a sustaining love, neither of them able to renew their vows, not even able to delay destruction for a few months. Like a receding tide, their love had only left debris behind. The only thing I had to determine was how to present this drama of emptiness, parallel to the mystery of the murders in the embassy.

I waited for the next words, the next sentence, the next paragraph.

Nothing arrived.

One hour went by, then another, then one more, and no words came to the rescue, or the words that did come were pathetic and bland and uninspired and the pieces of paper on which they had left their shitty black marks had been shamefully consigned to the trash basket—

I blamed my paralysis on any number of reasons, but kept pushing away a nagging doubt as to whether there was not something more fundamental, structural, that blocked my writing. Or was it that I dared not risk being left without a creative lifeboat, adrift, shipwrecked on the rocks of the treacherous Chilean transition, with no project to fill my days, no refuge against the void of silence and solitude?

No, it could not be that.

Maybe I needed to figure out the plot. Hadn't I read that the best mystery writers begin by pinpointing the culprit and, from there, adjust the story so the hero will be able to discover that identity, but not before a stream of red herrings and false clues have been liberally strewn to throw readers – and the detective – off the scent.

While I tried to puzzle this out – who could possibly be behind what seemed haphazard murders? - I also decided to find out what sort of work Antonio might have been engaged in if he had not followed his lover into the embassy, in fact the sort of cases that he would return to if he solved the current mysterious deaths and was rewarded with the chance to go back to his previous life. For that I accosted all manner of random Chileans on the street and in buses and shops, asking them if they might have heard about murders occurring in the chaotic aftermath of the coup, private crimes, vigilante justice run amok, unrelated to the military intervention itself.

The answers were intriguing. One old lady said she had heard of a jealous husband who had killed his promiscuous wife and dumped her in the river, to join the corpses of political prisoners floating there. A man selling trinkets from China was sure that a lad who went missing from a house down the block a week after the coup had been carved up by a neighbour and buried in his backyard as revenge for sleepless nights of incessant partying next door. A maid assured us that the young man in the house where she served had thrown his father down the stairs, blaming subversives, when it was clear that he wanted the inheritance to pay for his gambling debts. And a shopkeeper swore that a local businessman had hired a petty thug to bump off an emerging rival whose death nobody would investigate, as he was an Allende sympathiser. I felt quite satisfied: these examples, though probably urban legends, products of overly fertile imaginations, were precisely the sort of crimes that Antonio Coloma would have to explore if he abandoned the embassy to start run-of-the-mill homicide work, his investigations constantly blocked, lest they lead to some culprit high up in the military or civilian echelons of the regime. I wondered who would forbid my detective from carrying out his job? It had to be the head inspector of his brigade, a man I promptly baptised with the bizarre name of Anacleto Suárez, who was also Coloma's best buddy, someone who, I thought, might do anything to get his friend back, who –

Coloma's alarmed reaction signaled that he had seen those very marks before

And there it was, I suddenly knew who the murderer was, his motives, what devious manoeuvering had led to those homicides in the Embassy.

I began to breathlessly write what Antonio Coloma would narrate next:

"This way," the chargé d'affaires said, and by the humble way he spoke I knew that the power dynamic between us had drastically changed. Gone was the sneering tone that had characterised Neumann in the past—Neumann with two ns, he had said to me and Rachael when we had introduced ourselves to him, asking for asylum, two ns, he repeated, looking at Rachael's surname, Beckman, wouldn't want anybody to confuse his German ancestors with Jews— gone was that sense of superiority that came from knowing that he, the Aryan Hans Neumann, was the absolute arbiter of our fortune and the life and death of the other thousand refugees in the embassy, all of us at his mercy for food, bedding, sweaters, security, toothpaste, condoms, especially condoms, as he was quick to emphasise on that very first occasion.

Now this domesticated version of the sarcastic and malevolent Neumann took me gently by the arm and steered me down a corridor lined with mirrors, nodding fatuously at his own image as if he were a courtier walking through a gallery at Versailles, instead of a second-rate bureaucrat slithering along an underdeveloped imitation of some European palace. He came to a door framed in faux gold that, up till now, had always been locked, and extracting a set of jangling keys, proceeded to open it, revealing a toilet and shower inside. "My own private bathroom," he informed me, gesturing ceremoniously. And as if acknowledging that perhaps he had gone too far

in his obsequiousness: "Only this once."

I decided to take him down a peg, make him understand that I knew he needed my services more than I needed an exclusive place in which to piss: "Unless there's another murder," I said. "Then you'll have to share it with me again, eh? And with Rachael Beckman. With only one n."

"Surely you don't think that there will be a second—" but I did not wait for the rest of his reply, shut the door behind me and relieved myself with the joy of feeling that my dick was at least good for something. Confirmed a saying Suárez, my boss and best buddy, had regaled me with on the first day we worked together: "I don't believe in God, but when I piss, I believe in God."

My glee at remembering this joke disappeared as soon as I emerged from the bathroom and Neumann began to describe a salient feature of the body that he had omitted: on the forehead of the corpse the assailant had carved a circle that resembled a face, with a mouth and two eyes and a nose.

"A nose?" I asked in shock.

Neumann nodded. "Why? What's wrong?"

I paused in my furious typing. Because this revelation of what had been done to the victim further cemented my knowledge of who the murderer would be. Antonio Coloma's alarmed reaction signaled that he had seen those very marks before, during, I decided, three previous police inquiries well before the coup. The first time a year ago, when a circle in the corpse's face had been carved, along with the gape of a horribly smiling mouth. The second time, some months later, when Coloma and his team of detectives were called in to examine yet another body, which had the same circle and mouth, sporting, on this occasion, a left eye as well. And the last time—ah, the last time, a bare month or so ago, a third corpse with those same etchings, to which a right eye was added. Coloma would be puzzled, perhaps terrified, perhaps elated, by the fact that this body, just found by Neumann in the embassy, would have the same pattern etched on it, supplemented now with a nose, evidence that the serial killer he had been tracking down →

→ for the last year had struck inside the embassy, taking a fourth life with his malicious, sculpting hands. Unless it was a copycat. But my detective would quickly deduce that it could not be a copycat if so few people knew about that smiley face torturously engraved on the forehead of the victims. Among those few: Suárez and a couple of Coloma's former underlings at Investigaciones, and, of course, the son who had discovered his father's body that first time, and then the sister who had discovered her brother's body the second time, and as for the third and last one, with the mouth and the two eyes, it was a wife who had stumbled on it, a woman by the name of Rachael Beckman. Yes, that serial killer had inadvertently changed Coloma's life by introducing him to Rachael, turning her into a widow and my protagonist into a fugitive who, after the coup, had followed her to that infernal embassy in an act of irrevocable recklessness.

I wondered, along with Coloma, how Rachael would react when told that someone on these premises had mutilated a man with the same markings left on her assassinated husband? Would she panic if she thought the murderer was in the very place where she had sought sanctuary, would she begin to examine everyone with suspicion, the same suspicion now invading Coloma as he asked himself if the murderer was not one of the men who'd been in front or behind him in line just minutes earlier?

But it was too soon to explore these issues. Better to return to my detective as he walked with Neumann toward the scene of the crime—a gazebo at the far end of the colossal embassy garden, guarded by two employees (yes, that made sense) tasked with shooing away potential snoops with the pretext that the roof of the shelter

She hated her husband and would gladly have stabbed him, a reactionary pig, a fascist

was dangerously loose—better to concentrate on his thoughts:

"I tried to picture the body I was about to see, whether it was in the same position as the others, in the form of a crucifix, and if the mouth smiled in the same way, if the carved eyes were equally askew and glinting red, but another body invaded my mind, her body, Rachael's body, I couldn't avoid wondering if this discovery would make that body more accessible to me, open up to me again, as when I'd asked her to have a drink with me after her deposition, when she readily confessed over that whiskey and soda that she hated her husband and would gladly have stabbed him, a reactionary pig, a fascist, she said to me, not caring that this made her a suspect, not knowing that she couldn't be a suspect because she had an ironclad alibi for the first two murders, she had no idea that the man she had not lived with for years, that the husband she detested was the third in a series, no, she had spoken to me so frankly because she knew, as I knew, that we would make love that night—it was her body that mattered as I approached the corpse in the gazebo, that dead body that I hoped, perversely, would bring Rachael's living body closer to me, that this new murder would bring us together as that previous murder had. Or would it break us beyond repair?

Because . . .

And that was as far as I got, that "because" was where I stopped.

Because . . . because . . . I spent the next hours staring at the snow-white page jutting out of the Olivetti typewriter, trying to ignore the penetrating cold of my study, only looking up to watch the rain falling on Santiago as if it were the end of the world—and the end of my hopes for further inspiration.

* * *

I wonder if my obsession with the truncated characters, their lives brusquely interrupted, their aspirations consigned to dust is related to the *Desaparecidos*, the worst sort of punishment visited by the dictatorship on victims and those who loved them, harking back to when the Nazis vanished their enemies into the Nacht and Nebel, refusing a funeral to those they had murdered, I wonder if I am particularly attuned to these incomplete characters because I am surrounded by the ghosts of those abducted friends and comrades whose body I cannot visit, whose last minutes on Earth I know nothing about – are their bones bleaching underground or have they dissolved in the sea into which they may have been cast from a helicopter? So many decades watching the relatives of the missing searching for a femur or the sliver of a cranium to place in a grave, so many lives unconcluded, that remain open, so many presumed dead who cry out to be kept in our memory, brought back to some illusion of permanence, their deracinated life given finality?

The ones I cannot bring back.

Except that I could bring my characters back.

I could, but I don't, I haven't.

* * *

There I was, without the slightest inkling on how to continue.

This paralysis was all the more exacerbating because, from the moment Coloma recognised that the technique used in the embassy was that of the serial killer he had been pursuing, I knew exactly how the novel should end, the warped reasons behind this new string of homicides.

I'd call the murderer Raúl, for now at least, for convenience's sake until I found a more suitable and sinister name (or maybe best that it be innocuous) – after all, I hadn't worked out yet how Coloma would track Raúl down, gets him to confess that he committed four ritual assassinations in the embassy, which, added to the three he had already perpetrated earlier, the three unresolved murders that Coloma had been investigating when he was a police inspector, complete the magic number seven. Raúl's motives seem wild and apocalyptic. He claims to be a revolutionary, the only true one, the heir to Stalin, who has been speaking to him since Allende won the elections, demanding that

certain features be carved into seven bodies, eyes, mouth, nose, ears, and hair, until the face of God has been fully displayed, the face of Stalin and Jesus superimposed on those other faces, necessary sacrifices so that the society of the future can be born, so that Chileans can understand, the world can understand, that without blood there can be no real and radical transformation. Having completed his mission, Raúl is now ready to leave the embassy, give himself up to the authorities so they can execute him and insure his eternal resurrection.

I imagined how nonplussed readers would be. Not what they expected from an author like me, who had made a habit of attacking traditional narrative structures and what could be more traditional than this climax, a triumphant detective single-handedly defusing the ticking diplomatic time bomb, the author resorting to a psychopath, reducing terrible transgressions to insanity? Instead of making us question a corrupt system like the best noir thrillers.

But there was a twist, a trick I was playing on both Coloma and my readers. My novel had plenty of corruption, was noir to the core. As soon as Raúl was taken into custody, Coloma receives a phone call from his old friend Suárez, the head of the detective division. The military, appreciating that Coloma's intervention has averted war between Chile and Argentina, has granted him a full amnesty. He can return to active duty, get his old life back. So Coloma breaks with Rachael, is embraced affectionately by wife and child, and the next day shows up at headquarters, where Suárez informs him that the number one priority is to catch the serial killer who has continued his gruesome murders, striking several times while Coloma, as well as Raúl, have been in the embassy.

What? Hadn't Raúl confessed, doesn't he know what nobody else knows, how the first three bodies were defaced, it would be farfetched to suggest he's been leaving the embassy to kill more and then sneaking back in. But that's not the answer. In fact, Raúl has been an undercover agent for the military since way before the coup. As he had infiltrated one of   →

→ the revolutionary organisations, he's the perfect person to seek asylum in Coloma's embassy when Suárez requires someone in it to start bumping off refugees using the very techniques of the madman still at large. Concentrate, Suárez told Raúl, on the most violent, dangerous, fevered. You'll be doing the country a service, ridding us of the terrorists we'll have to dispatch at some point, save us the trouble, my boy. Succeed in this operation and you've quite a career in front of you. Promising Raúl that, like all of Pinochet's henchmen, he won't be put on trial, but promoted, given a medal, sent on to work with the secret police.

All of which was organised by Suárez for one purpose. When you sought asylum, Suárez tells Coloma, I asked myself how to save you from your own folly, get my best detective and best friend back here, solving crimes and drinking wine with me. Only way: to make you feel

personally challenged by a criminal who, having escaped detection all these months out there, now taunts you in the place you've escaped to. I instructed Raúl to leave behind just the right amount of breadcrumbs to guarantee that he'd be caught, so you could abandon the embassy, resume your life, and hunt down the original serial killer.

By the dark and crooked ending of the novel, Coloma has, therefore, learned something about himself: that he's spent his career chasing minor monsters, while the major ones, the big fish that rule the world, are beyond justice.

My only problem now was how to get to that final moment.

Because I was still paralysed with doubt.

When I had set out to write this novel, originally, back in October of 1973, and all through the years that ensued, I had thought of the embassy as a secluded temple of safety and

freedom in a Chile gone mad with violence. My detective was reestablishing order in the universe by discovering the transgressor, the basic premise of most detective stories since the very beginning of the genre, what's so satisfying and comforting about them – and comforting when I first came up with the idea. Barbarism reigns everywhere in the country, but in this one small haven there's a semblance of justice, the hope that someday a similar justice might be meted out beyond the constricted boundaries of the embassy, no crimes going unpunished.

But here I was in 1990s Chile and its restricted democracy: that prophetic idea that justice will finally be done, so entrancing and promising during the Pinochet years, mocks us in this ravaged land where the criminals are immune from prosecution, protected by a commander in chief who threatens to come roaring back with the same tanks and planes that attacked and destroyed the presidential palace on September 11th if anyone dares to touch even the pinky finger of any of his accomplices, even dares to name them. So we know who the culprits are, but they're exempt from the laws that govern their fellow citizens, free to stroll the alamedas, the avenues full of trees that, in his last speech, before he committed suicide or was murdered, Allende had predicted would open for the free men of tomorrow. But it turns out that the torturers are the only ones who are truly free, the rest of us are fucked. Maybe my novel should really start when Coloma leaves the embassy and has to face the truth about the society he's supposedly defending, the complex world outside. But that's not the murder mystery I set out to write.

A question I had not dared ask surfaced without my knowing how to answer it: Was it the wrong time for this novel?

A question I once again dismissed.

Wrong time or not, I was determined not to forsake Coloma. Last time I connected with him, he had left his urinal and was about to find out the identity of the first body, perhaps one of the ultra-extremists he'd come to detest, a real asshole, full of delusions and hot air, perhaps an older, gentle, calm man who's participated in

other failed revolutions across Latin America. Whoever it is, Coloma will have to face the death of someone close to him, I'd have to face that death, that pain. It would be a cop-out to avoid that pain or another sort of pain, his and mine, when he realises he's losing Rachael, watching her unravel, grow ever more distant, and not to know how to reach across the abyss between them and heal her broken life. Leaving him unfinished, I'd never forgive myself. And he'd never forgive me. No way was I going to kill off Antonio Coloma.

The ferocity of my reaction gave me the impulse to proceed, once again the words visited me, I knew what came next, Antonio and me, together, we would defeat this silence, I would not disrespect him.

I had left him ready to be shocked by the identity of the first body, but unable to concentrate with the usual professionalism he brought to crime scenes. All he could think about was Rachael, the need to madly make love to her. Maybe he could pressure the surprisingly pliant Neumann, that hellhound *chargé d'affaires*, to find a secluded, plush room where he and Rachael could explore each other without the prying ears and heaving bodies of all those couples inside sleeping bags on the hard oak floor of the ballroom.

So far, so good. Either my couple's carnal appetite or my erotic imagination had me on the right track. Except that when I burrowed into Coloma's feverish envisioning of what he and Rachael would do if they were alone, as he anticipated with fruition the details of that lovemaking, her anatomy and skin and fake coyness and utter brashness as she hid her breasts and revealed them, hid each opening in her body and revealed it, I ran into trouble. Or maybe it was him, my detective, who was in trouble, beset by unforeseen and terrible images? Because what kept corroding his imagination, what came to his mind, what came to my mind, was the ravaged body of someone who had been tortured and raped.

No, I said to Coloma, you're wrong. That's precisely the fate your lover escaped by seeking asylum, the sort of atrocity that threatens other →

I hear her say: Promise you'll find him, promise me

→ women on the other side of the wall that shields the embassy. You would never destroy your brilliant career, leave your family, for someone that wounded. What attracted you was her free relationship with her body, the promise to do with it what she willed, not subject to male hands or desires. Rachael had been conceived as an unbridled, inviolate, magnificently liberated female in total control of her vagina.

She was as far from a rape victim as she could conceivably be. I had met far too many of those damaged women during my exile and, on returning to Chile for seven months in 1986, had worked with a team of psychologists treating that trauma. I was still haunted by the silence those former female prisoners foundered in, the lasting, irreparable damage. On the few occasions when some words could be coaxed from them about their ordeal, they spoke in short, impassive sentences, they never met my eyes, finally withdrew into some territory inside the confines of their mind. Impossible to know, better not to know, what they were thinking, what cellars and attics they continued to inhabit, the scars and screams that continued to echo in their memory. No, I said to Rachael, I created you as someone entirely different, a cross between Bizet's Carmen and La Pasionaria, militant and erotic, playful in sex and serious in politics. No, I said to Coloma, I will not let our Rachael, the symbol of an insurgent, uninhibited Chile that I still hold dear, journey into that darkness.

I wrote:

Coloma thought of a soft bed that he could wangle out of Neumann in exchange for help in solving this murder, imagined Rachael's hand as she patted the pillow, her smile as she inhaled the smell of clean sheets, invited him to unfasten her blouse, he had not seen her naked since they had asked for asylum, maybe they could find each

other again in this very embassy, maybe they'd have to wait till they left this overcrowded place thick with the stench of scores of unwashed residents, when they could shower every day and feed each other morsels of succulent meals and spend days exploring a city like Paris and nights exploring a continent called Rachael.

But as soon as I had finished describing Coloma's anticipation of the delights of that continent called Rachael, what stubbornly surged in my mind next hadn't the slightest romantic resonance.

What I saw, even if I did not want to, was Rachael holding back tears of rage, Coloma saw, even if he did not want to, a woman who refused to undress in front of any man, had no tolerance for sensual games, resented the pillow, the clean sheets, the promises of a marvelous future, all of it false, all of it imposed on her, ignoring who she really was.

Find him, I hear Rachael say to Coloma.

Find him? The murderer?

No. Him. The man who did this to me.

Did what to you?

I eavesdrop on them, I watch them disobey my plans for them, refuse to collaborate, I listen to Rachael speaking in a way that is miles away from everything I knew about her, I hear her say: Promise you'll find him, promise me.

And Coloma answers, I promise, I promise a day will come when that man will be standing in front of you and your eyes will be able to roam over his face, I promise you a day will come when justice will be done.

I'll hold you to that promise, my love.

As for me, the supposed writer of this novel, I am astonished at this development. What are they talking about, who is that man she wants to track down, that Coloma has promised to find?

Rachael is unrecognisable. It's as if a stranger has taken over her life, dictated those words, turned her into . . . into whom? Who is it inside her, inside me, that demands to be heard?

And then, it comes to me, I remember another character in another novel, abandoned long ago, an abused female prisoner I'd called Paulina in a work begun in the bleak winter of exile and never

finished, that is who Rachael reminds me of.

Paulina. Obsessed with one of the men who had tortured her, specifically a doctor—a man who had sworn an oath to heal people—presiding over those sessions under the pretext of keeping her alive, using the occasion to repeatedly rape the woman he should have been protecting. I had decided that Paulina would stumble across that man by accident, recognise him as her tormentor, entice him to her home, where she'd hold him hostage. And that was as far as I'd gone, never sallied beyond the first pages, bogged down by too many unanswered questions. Did I focus exclusively on that woman seeking revenge or did I also bring in the police combing a terrorised city for the whereabouts of the kidnapped doctor? Was she alone in her quest or did she have, it made sense, a husband—or maybe it was her lover?—a father, a brother, some male figure in any case, bent on violently restoring the family

honour, who was he? And why would Paulina recklessly take justice into her own hands when there was hope that a return to democracy would lead to trials, why not wait for that day?

Overburdened with such unresolvable dilemmas, I had let that novel lapse, promised Paulina I'd return to her when the time was right. I make such promises to all the unfulfilled characters I reluctantly desert, even if I doubt I'll bring them back from the dust of distance to which they've been relegated.

And yet, Paulina had evidently remained alive, remembered my promise from some recess inside me, here she was, still struggling to come out, speaking from Rachael's lips, from inside Rachael's throat. Did that mean that the moment had come for me to resurrect her? Was that what Rachael was trying to tell me?

Because it now seemed obvious that I had made a mistake by placing Paulina's quest →

→ during dictatorial times. It was in contemporary Chile that she belonged, it was a contorted transition that, by dashing her hopes that the man who raped and tortured her would be brought to justice, forced her to take the law into her own hands. Kidnapping that doctor and putting him on trial in her home was a protest against a country that, in the name of the public good, was demanding that she forget what had been inflicted on her, a country that was silencing her, betraying her, sacrificing her on the altar of peace and reconciliation. And what if, what if, what if her husband is on the Truth Commission that the new democratic government has established to investigate cases that ended in death, but not the living dead, who are still suffering the traumas of the recent past, investigating the *desaparecidos* but not victims like Paulina? How would that ambitious lawyer respond to his wife tormenting and perhaps murdering someone whose guilt is not evident, the only proof a deranged blur of memories from a woman who will do anything to be rid of her nightmares and grievances? Would he not see that act of hers as insane, politically irresponsible, creating an impossible predicament for him, for the Commission, for a precariously balanced government, upsetting the delicate pact that stipulates that we get back our democracy as long as we accept that none of the perpetrators are to be held to account, never named?

And the more I delved into what it would mean to transfer Paulina's story to 1990, the more I had to admit what I had not wanted to admit as I fruitlessly tried to write my Embassy Murders novel, admit now that there was no way I could spend my time and energy on Coloma's search for a serial killer in a padlocked building full of failed revolutionaries, no way that such a novel could address the most intriguing and anguishing situation that Chile was facing and that demanded to be expressed. Not how to change ourselves in the urgent aftermath of the coup so we could forge the right alliance to get rid of Pinochet, but how to survive the indefinite aftermath of his reign with our ethics intact. How to build a country of truth if perpetrators and victims coexisted in the same space, crossed each

other on the same streets, in cafés and concerts, and lied about how easy that would be, lied that it would not corrupt our soul? How to reconcile oneself to the certainty that full justice had not, could not be done?

But a novel did not seem the best vehicle to deal with these issues. What the country needed was a play, a public act of catharsis that compelled us to look at ourselves in a mirror and see who we were, all of us gathered under one roof in one dark hall. Not readers of fiction enclosed in private worlds, not isolated, anonymous individuals, but an audience forced to digest the performance together and later debate the intractable dilemmas with one another. The public space of the theatre prolonged into, and representative of, the larger public space of the nation.

I could see it in my head, the first scene, Paulina curled up like a fetus under the moonlight, next to the sea, at a beach house, waiting for her husband to come home and tell her if he was to head the Commission, it took possession of me as nothing had done before.

And as I followed my Paulina and her husband and the doctor she thought had raped and betrayed her, I felt that I was writing myself into relevance again, intervening in the history of my country as I had so often dreamed when I was in exile. What better way to participate in the search and struggle for the soul of our land, what better way to prove I belonged here?

* * *

As I grow older, I look towards the many characters I started and left by the wayside, I know that, as I fade, so will they, and I cannot but wonder is there one I should bring back to life, is there one I promised to revivify and never did, is there one from whom I need to ask forgiveness?

* * *

And thus it was that, after having spent so many hours with Antonio Coloma, I jettisoned him, did not even grant him the reprieve of a funeral or a

Now I had aborted him, left him alone in the dark

farewell ceremony. In order to assuage the sorrow of this separation, the pangs of guilt stabbing me, I lied to him, really to myself, I'll get back to you, just like I returned to Paulina, can't you see? . . . lied to him as I put away the pages that had given him birth, to which no further pages would be added. I had nursed him as one would a recently born child, checking in on him periodically to see if he was still breathing, if he was eating well and was not cold at night, fretting over every detail, creating a whole back story for him and plans for his investigation, and now I had aborted him, left him alone in the dark, waiting for completion, wondering why I, his best friend and only family, had done this to him.

I worry, nevertheless, that I may be overdramatising what happened between Coloma and me, giving that relationship with my character a supreme importance it never really had. Because Antonio is not as alone in that darkness as I have depicted him, not the only one to suffer that desertion. Today, thirty years later, as old age is upon me, my drawers overflow with stories and novels and plays and poems, so many projects I started and that will never be taken up again, that will die when, soon enough, their imperfect author breathes his last. But at least those creatures of mine will expire not out of a deliberate act of betraying them but because my time is also running out. They will not be the victims of a homicide, like Coloma's was—yes, his consignment to oblivion was like murder, except there is no one to investigate the crime, nobody to pursue the murderer or seek justice for the victim.

I regret that I did not give myself the time back then to mourn his loss. I was too absorbed in the wonder of the new universe that awaited discovery and that, unlike the embassy novel, was offering no stuttering resistance to being conceived, seemed to be writing itself as if dictated by Paulina, as if she were possessing me as she had possessed Rachael and spoken through her mouth.

Did Antonio Coloma, as he faded, resent this abandonment, reproach me for breaking the vow that I would be true to him till death did us part?

More generous would be to suggest that my friend Antonio approved of my choice, the necessity of his own passing so somebody more crucial and inspiring, another fictitious character, could take his place in my affections, maybe he is like a wife who dies after having selected the ideal mate for her husband and blesses that union from beyond the grave. Perhaps he would have told me, if I had consulted him, that continuing to plunge into the post-coup world of the embassy was a way of evading the responsibilities of the present. Don't you want, he might have said to me, to be different from your compatriots, so massively engaged in averting their gaze from reality?

Oh, Antonio, you did not deserve to be disappeared like this, you should have found a better author to take care of you.

* * *

He would disagree.

Maybe he would point out that what he needed was a funeral, a passage from the transience of living to the permanence of ancestral death.

Maybe the reason why I write this now, as I approach my own ending, is to provide, at least in words, this literary urn where he can rest, this simulacrum of completion.

Maybe this is my way of asking for forgiveness, my way of imagining that he grants it, smiles at me unfadingly from the Land of the Unfinished and wishes me well on my own journey. ✖

Ariel Dorfman is the Chilean-American author of Death and the Maiden and the forthcoming novel, The Suicide Museum, from which this story is adapted

52(03):98/119 | DOI:10.1177/03064220231201323

Lines of inquiry

Index speaks to **RICHARD NORTON-TAYLOR** who has reported
on some of the biggest government scandals over the past four decades

AS FORMER DEFENSE and security correspondent for The Guardian, Richard Norton-Taylor has been at the heart of the biggest stories to hit UK headlines for 40 years. One former official called Norton-Taylor a "long-term thorn in the side of the intelligence establishment". He has written plays based on high-profile public inquiries, such as the one into Stephen Lawrence's murder, and has a new book out, The State of Secrecy.

INDEX Do you worry about the media's ability to hold the powerful to account?

RICHARD NORTON-TAYLOR Investigative journalism takes time and money and the reporter is not coming out with a story every day. Far too many editors, apart from perhaps at Private Eye and the Guardian, underestimate the interest in stories uncovering what is being done by so-called public institutions and by governments wasting taxpayers' money.

INDEX Have things changed with the security services since you first started writing about them?

R N-T They learned the very, very hard way. In the late 80s the European Court of Human Rights had a case brought by the National Council of Civil Liberties, now Liberty, and they said that bugging without any legal control at all, without any accountability, was unlawful. This forced the British Government to at least put MI5 on a legal footing. Some of the victories came as courts and the judges became increasingly understanding of our attempts to persuade MI5 and MI6 to account for themselves.

INDEX It's hard for a leopard to change its spots though, right?

R N-T There were stories for a long time about MI6 involvement which said they were conniving with the CIA on the rendition and subsequent torture of Libyans [in the early 2000s]. They finally did admit their role in it and paid compensation. After 9-11, there were a number of British residents who had sent been sent to Guantanamo Bay and were demanding compensation. There was an admission by the British intelligence services that they helped to the CIA and others to incarcerate them. Yet the Government then introduced the Justice and Security Act of 2013 which set up a new series of secret courts. It has nothing to do with justice at all. It just prevents us by statute from getting information out of the intelligence agencies.

INDEX What's your view on the value of public inquiries?

R N-T A lot of information comes out. The editors will have a story the first day and maybe when the verdict comes they will have another story... Take Grenfell, and the stories of who was to blame, the outrageous behaviour and excuses by companies, the behaviour of officials and police officers, and so on. Index: Do whistleblowers still want to come forward?

R N-T It's getting increasingly difficult. We see the NHS, for example, putting pressure on whistleblowers and potential whistleblowers. It is a question of trust and you've got to build that up. Over a very long period they would test the water and give you stories and see how you published them. If you didn't embarrass them, they would give you more stories. The government is trying to push through more and more secretive laws, new attempts at surveillance and new police powers. They are picking up people they regard as threats to national security, whether they're your potential sources as a journalist, or even journalists themselves."

INDEX What are your thoughts on the government's plans to stop end-to-end encryption?

R N-T Ministers have been swayed by the intelligence agencies to push for this and they think that end-to-end encryption prevents us from handling genuine threats to national security, not just paedophiles. GCHQ has complained saying it's increasingly difficult to find the needle in the haystack. I say actually they're building more and more haystacks because of the temptation to pursue and to maintain systems of mass surveillance and keeping hold of personal information and communications because one day it may be useful.

INDEX If you were detained and had to take one book to jail with you, what would it be?

R N-T I think James Joyce's Ulysses or George Eliot's Middlemarch.

INDEX What news headline would you most like to read?

R N-T "The UK abolishes the Official Secrets Act to set an example to the rest of the world". The subhead would be "Introduces robust law to protect whistleblowers". ✖

52(03):120/120|DOI:010.1177/03064220231201324

Printed in the USA
CPSIA information can be obtained
at www.ICGtesting.com
JSHW070828120224
57162JS00014B/242